on track ...
QUEEN

every album, every song

Andrew Wild

Sonicbond Publishing Limited
www.sonicbondpublishing.co.uk
Email: info@sonicbondpublishing.co.uk

First Published in the United Kingdom 2018
First Published in the United States 2019

British Library Cataloguing in Publication Data:
A Catalogue record for this book is available from the British Library

Copyright Andrew Wild 2018

ISBN 978-1-78952-003-3

Typset in ITC Garamond & Berthold Akzidenz Grotesk
Printed and bound in England

Graphic design and typesetting: Full Moon Media

For Stuart Nicholson, a fan and a pal

The 'Thank You' List:

To Stacy Doller and Mike Pollack, for filling the gaps in my collection
– listen to their shows at www.progzilla.com;
To Peter Hince for his time in answering many email queries;
To Steve Pilkington, editor to the stars;
To Julian Cox, captain camera;
To Simon Godfrey, Andy Sears, Stuart Nicholson, Lee Abraham,
Peter Munro, Kelvin Papp, Peter Jones and Lee Dudley
for suggestions and support;
To Sam Smyth and Anthony Rowsick, my lovely proof-readers;
To Stephen Lambe, for patience, humour, boundless enthusiasm
and ongoing belief in what we are trying to achieve;
To Huw Lloyd-Jones;
To Rosie and Amy;
And, of course, to Amanda, whose idea it was.

Contents

Introduction

Queen. Love them or hate them, everyone has an opinion. Everyone knows their music. From the radio-friendly hit singles to the early prog rock epics, from the cod-heavy bombast to the jazz pastiches, from the introspective ballads to the thumping anthems, Queen's music continues to be heard all around the world.

Queen were already a hugely successful band when, in July 1985, they were the outstanding act at the Live Aid concert in London, surely the biggest popular culture event of the '80s and voted the greatest live performance of all time in 2005. Their subsequent tour – 26 massive shows to over a million people across Europe during summer 1986 – secured their legendary status. Yet, none of this would have happened without the writing and performing skills of Freddie Mercury. Even the most technically-adept musicians need a writer and front-man. And in Freddie Mercury – flamboyant, eccentric, enigmatic, literate, camp, colourful – Queen were blessed with one of the best performers in rock. Perhaps *the* best.

The two key elements for Queen's unique sound should, at face value, be mutually incompatible. Firstly, Queen intelligently combined hard rock, prog rock, opera, music hall and power ballads with overblown vocal and guitar arrangements. In this respect they are a 'clever' band, an arty band, if you like. Secondly, Queen are accessible – their songs are short, often commercial and great to sing along with (witness all those hit singles), but can be unsubtle, direct, to-the-point. Almost artless. How can an 'arty' band be 'artless'? You tell me, but they were.

Queen have never been 'hip' – they appealed to the masses and this makes rock critics unnecessarily snooty. Many contemporary reviews were savage, including one notorious write-up that compared 'We Will Rock You' with a Nazi rally cry:

This group has come to make it clear exactly who is superior and who is inferior. Its anthem, 'We Will Rock You', is a marching order: you will not rock us, we will rock you. Indeed, Queen may be the first truly fascist rock band. The whole thing makes me wonder why anyone would indulge these creeps and their polluting ideas.
Dave Marsh, Rolling Stone, 8 February 1979

As Dominique Leone wrote in Pitchfork in 2011: 'For all their reported bombast, pomp, and tendency to overshoot and double-slaughter any semblances of good taste, everything you've heard about them is still true. They're one of the few phenomena who deliver on the hype, regardless of how you approach them.'

And it is easy and convenient to categorise Queen's history into two eras: before Freddie Mercury's death and afterwards. Whilst it's true that, over the last 25 years or more, Brian May and Roger Taylor have very much capitalised on the music that Queen made between 1973 and 1991, that legacy is beloved still by millions of people.

This book examines Queen's music, album by album, song by song, in detail. Where possible, recourse to the original multi-track master tapes has provided extra insight. The familiar hits are revisited, but those classic album cuts – 'The Night Comes Down', 'Liar', 'The March of the Black Queen', 'Brighton Rock', 'Death on Two Legs', 'The Prophet's Song', 'Love of my Life', 'You Take My Breath Away', 'The Millionaire Waltz', 'Dragon Attack', 'Bijou', 'Mother Love', 'My Fairy King', 'Nevermore', 'Love Of My Life', 'You and I', 'It's Late', 'It's a Beautiful Day', 'My Melancholy Blues', 'Is This the World We Created...?' – are given equal precedence.

Queen had strength in depth. These are the songs on which a legend was built.

Andrew Wild
Rainow, Cheshire, 2018
andrewwild.progzilla.com

What is included and what is not included

This book revisits, examines, analyses and describes each track from Queen's fifteen studio albums, from their self-titled debut released in 1973 to *Made in Heaven* in 1995. Any contemporary non-album tracks, B-sides and known unreleased songs are also included. Common variants such as single mixes, radio sessions and remixes are listed, along with live performance details. For details of Queen's many live releases and DVDs, I recommend the excellent website www.ultimatequeen.co.uk.

Promo singles, international variants, bootleg recordings, unreleased demos of released songs and solo material are not included unless they have a specific impact on a released song by Queen – readers are directed to the exhaustive *The Queen Chronology* (Patrick Lemieux and Adam Unger, 2013) and to the websites www.queenvault.com, www.queenzone.com and www.ultimatequeen.co.uk for full details of these.

A concluding chapter discusses the post-Freddie years, including: new songs in 1997, 2003 and 2014; *The Cosmos Rocks*; and the band's tours with Paul Rodgers and with Adam Lambert.

1970–1974: As It Began

Queen were never the most conventional of rocks stars. Brian May ... the erudite, earnest and academic guitar virtuoso. John Deacon ... the archetypal non-singing bassist who wrote both a four-to-the-floor disco-funk classic and one of the greatest karaoke anthems of the 20th century. The secret weapon in the band's song writing arsenal. Roger Taylor ... the dynamic drummer, singer of immense power and range, and the other secret weapon in the band's song writing arsenal. And Freddie Mercury ... the lead vocalist and front-man who provided the charisma, extravagance, swagger, musical chops and damn-it-all bravado. And who wrote hit after hit after hit.

Individually they were talented musicians and songwriters with rare depth, each with a keen ear for a catchy melody: all four of the band wrote top ten hit singles. Collectively, and especially on stage, Queen were an unstoppable force of nature.

Throughout their history, Queen operated exclusively on their own terms. That history starts in 1963, when 16-year old Brian May built a guitar with his father.

May (born 19 July 1947, Hampton, Middlesex), formed his first band in 1964 with schoolmate Tim Staffell. The band, blues-rock in style, was named 1984 and continued to perform after both May and Staffell left school and went to further education in London: May to Imperial College with a £75 per annum scholarship and Staffell to Ealing College of Art, about 40 minutes on the Tube from central London. 1984 disbanded in spring 1968 when May graduated with a degree in physics. Their high point had been supporting the Jimi Hendrix Experience at Imperial College.

'I was on the Entertainments Committee at Imperial College in West London who booked Jimi in May 1967,' May told *Loudersound* in 2015. 'It was a sort of ball: you had three or four groups playing in different parts of the building. We were playing in a room at the bottom, and Jimi was on in the main hall so, yes, in a sense, we supported him. I remember, we were stood in the little corridor backstage between the stage and Jimi's dressing room – just kind of clumped outside waiting for him. Jimi came out of the dressing room and said: "Where's the stage, man?" We just pointed [starstruck]. He was the coolest guy on earth. No doubt about it. We played 'Purple Haze' that night as a kind of tribute to Jimi, and it's rumoured that he came down and saw me playing it. People have told me that he came in, stood at the back and watched. I had no idea.'

May and Staffell decided to form a new band, and an advertisement on the college notice board brought them medical student and drummer Roger Taylor.

Taylor (born 26 July 1949, King's Lynn, Norfolk) had grown up in Cornwall, and formed his first serious band, Beat Unlimited, in 1963. Taylor played with many bands in Cornwall including the Cousin Jacks, and Johnny Quayle and the Reactions. He moved to London in October 1967. His flatmate studied at Imperial College and, in autumn 1968, saw a postcard pinned to a noticeboard: 'Ginger Baker / Mitch Mitchell-style drummer wanted'.

May, Taylor and Staffell called their new band Smile, played their first gig in October 1968 and signed to Mercury records in 1969.

Tim Staffell was a student at Ealing with 22-year old Farrokh Bulsara. Bulsara, known to all as 'Freddie' had been born on 5 September 1946 in Zanzibar to Indian parents and had moved to Feltham, Middlesex, a few miles west of London, in 1964. He started at Ealing in 1966.

'I went to Ealing Art School a year after Pete Townshend left,' Freddie told Caroline Coon in 1974. 'Music was a side-line to everything we did. The school was a breeding ground for musicians.' [1]

After becoming friendly with Staffell, Bulsara became a follower of Smile and made first contact with Brian May and Roger Taylor.

Smile recorded three tracks at Trident Studios that June. The resulting single, 'Earth' (Staffell) backed with 'Step on Me' (Staffell/May), failed to attract any attention. Through a sister of a girlfriend of a friend, Smile and their friend Freddie were introduced to a band from St Helens called Ibex. The core trio in Ibex – guitarist Mike Bersin, drummer Mick Smith and bassist John Taylor – had decided to try their luck in London and needed a singer. Keen to perform, and determined to succeed, Freddie joined Ibex in August 1969. His nickname in the band was Ponce.

Freddie in 1974: 'I got my diploma and then I thought I'd chance it as a freelance artist. I tried. I did it for a couple of months, but I'd done it for so long I thought, "My God, I've done enough." The interest wasn't there. And the music thing just grew and grew. Finally, I said, "Right, I'm taking the plunge, it's music." I'm one of those people believes in doing those things which interest you. Music is so interesting, dear.' [2]

Ibex would play covers by bands such as Led Zeppelin, Cream, Muddy Waters, Yes and Jimi Hendrix. A live recording of the Beatles' song 'Rain' was officially released on *The Solo Collection* in 2000.

Smile recorded three more songs at De Lane Lea Studios in September 1969. Ibex, meanwhile, changed their name to Wreckage in October 1969 and recorded some demos at this time – one song called 'Green' has been officially released. Despite playing a few gigs at Ealing College, Wreckage would disband before the end of 1969. Freddie spent about eight weeks in another band called Sour Milk Sea in February and April 1970.

Frustrated by lack of progress, Smile broke up in late February 1970. Brian May and Roger Taylor, always ambitious, continued to plan future projects. Their close friend Freddie Bulsara was brought into the discussions.

Queen was formed in April 1970: Freddie Bulsara, Brian May, Roger Taylor and bassist Mike Grose, an old friend of Roger Taylor's from Truro. Queen might well have been named Grand Dance (Brian's suggestion), or the Rich Kids (Roger's). Freddie's suggestion, Queen, initially made the others laugh, then recoil in alarm. But then it was short and memorable. Queen it would be. Shortly afterwards Freddie Bulsara would rename himself Freddie Mercury: preposterous but somehow right.

13

The new band performed their first gig in Truro on 27 June 1970, billed as Smile, a long-promised charity fundraiser for Taylor's mother. Their first concert as Queen took place at Imperial College in London on 12 July 1970. Early original songs include 'Keep Yourself Alive', 'Liar', 'Son and Daughter' and 'Stone Cold Crazy', with a few carried over from Ibex, Wreckage and Smile.

Mike Grose was replaced by Barry Michell (August 1970 to January 1971) and Doug Bogie (February 1971), then by nineteen-year-old John Deacon. Deacon (born 19 August 1951, Leicester) was a student at Chelsea College and had seen Queen perform in October 1970. He was introduced to May and Taylor by a mutual friend in early 1971, after Doug Bogie had left the band. By late February 1971 the pieces of the Queen jigsaw had found each other.

'We certainly have an ingredient between the four of us otherwise it wouldn't have worked, especially for this long,' Freddie told Rudi Dolezal in 1984. 'We all have a role to play, but I couldn't tell you what it was. We're diverse, we're four different characters … no two of us are the same … we all like totally different things, but we come together, it's a chemistry that works. It's just something that seems to fit, and that's what good bands are made of, you know? And we're good.'

They would stay together for almost 21 years.

'A simple plan,' wrote Mike West in one of the earliest Queen histories. 'To package good tunes with exciting playing and serve it up with flair and a fashionable image, thereby hitting the heavy rock fans squarely in the gut, the pop fans in the ear, and captivating the teenyboppers with flash and glamour.' [3]

Queen's early years are particularly well-documented by Mark Blake in his excellent book *Is This the Real Life?* (2010).

Queen (1973)

Personnel:
Freddie Mercury: vocals, piano, Hammond organ
Brian May: guitar, piano, vocals
Roger Taylor (credited as 'Roger Meddows-Taylor'): drums, percussion, vocals, lead vocals
John Deacon (credited as 'Deacon John'): bass guitar
+ John Anthony: backing vocals on 'Modern Times Rock 'n' Roll'.
Recorded in December 1971, and between June and November 1972 at De Lane Lea and Trident Studios, London. Produced by John Anthony, Roy Thomas Baker and Queen.
UK release date: 13 July 1973. US release date: 4 September 1973.
Highest chart places: UK: 24, US 83. [4]

Queen, the band, had an extended false start. The band had been together for almost two years when they were invited to test out the recording facilities at De Lane Lea Studios in Wembley, London. Brian May had called an old contact Terry Yeadon, who had engineered the second Smile session in 1969.

Yeadon had just relocated De Lane Lea from central London and wanted to test the studio. May's fortuitous call, in around September 1971, resulted in an invitation to Queen to record a demo in a professional studio. That December Queen recorded sixteen-track demos of five songs: 'Keep Yourself Alive', 'The Night Comes Down', 'Great King Rat', 'Jesus' and 'Liar'. All of these were released on the 2011 re-issue of *Queen* – they are remarkably polished.

Still keen to sign a decent record deal, the band used the tape to entice record companies. Eventually, they were given a break by Barry and Norman Sheffield, owners of Trident Studios in Soho. Previous customers at Trident included the Beatles ('Hey Jude' and parts of the *White Album*), George Harrison (*All Things Must Pass*) and David Bowie (*Hunky Dory* and *The Rise and Fall of Ziggy Stardust*). The Sheffields had been alerted to Queen by John Anthony, who had been Smile's A&R manager at Mercury Records.

'I was sitting in my office one day in 1971,' wrote Norman Sheffield in his memoirs, 'when I got a call from my brother Barry down in the studio. 'Norman, come down and have a listen to something,' he said. John Anthony, Trident's A&R man, had discovered a band called Smile. At the start, the lead guitarist was an astrophysics student from Imperial College called Brian May, the bassist and singer was an art student called Tim Staffell, and the drummer was a biology student called Roger Taylor. It turned out that they'd now reshaped the band. Staffell had been replaced by this little Indian-looking guy with a big, operatic voice and they had a new bass player. John had asked for their demo. It was raw but there was definitely something there.'

The band were duly signed to a management deal with Trident and, without a record deal yet, they commenced the recording of their debut album over six months from June to December 1972.

'I agreed to offer the Queenies, as we christened them, a loose kind of arrangement,' wrote Norman Sheffield. 'There were times when the studio was 'dark', usually at 2am. So, we said: 'We'll give you this downtime in the studio to see what you can do.' They turned out to be every bit as good – and demanding – as we'd anticipated. Things had to be one hundred per cent right, otherwise they wouldn't be happy. They'd spend days and nights working on the harmonies.'

''Keep Yourself Alive', 'Liar', 'Great King Rat', and the other numbers are songs that we just used to play,' John Deacon told *Innerview* in 1977. 'And we just went in and recorded them. And there were one or two numbers on that first album which were more sort of that first sort of sign of getting interested in doing things in the studio.'

The album was co-produced by John Anthony with Trident colleague Roy Thomas Baker. Baker would become an important part of the Queen sound, co-producing five of their albums in the 1970s.

Trident eventually found British and American record labels who were interested in the band several months after album was completed. Queen were finally signed by EMI in March 1973, and by Elektra Records soon afterwards.

'I heard the [first] Queen album and I absolutely loved it,' says Electra boss Jac Holzman. 'It was like a beautifully cut jewel, landing in your lap, ready to go.'

Queen's debut album was released in mid-July 1973, seven months after its completion.

Brian May's view, in August 1973: 'We like some of the stuff on it, but we sometimes fell into the trap of over-arrangement. You know, the songs changed over the years and some of them probably evolved too much. You can get so far into something that you forget what the song originally was. On a personal level, it was frustrating for me to take so long to get to this point. I wanted to record things with, for instance, tape echoes and multiple guitars five years ago. Now I've finally done it, but in the meantime so have other people! Which is a bit disappointing.' [5]

Almost immediately after the release of the album, Queen went back into Trident Studios to record its follow-up.

This remarkable debut album stands out, in total, as a very bold move. Once you get past the Led Zeppelin-isms and push your tongue firmly into your cheek, here is a band with a very clear vision of what they wanted to say, and how they wanted to be heard. The confidence shines out.

Queen was ridiculous, catchy and a whole lot of fun.

'Keep Yourself Alive' (Brian May)

Released as a single a-side, 6 July 1973 (UK) and 9 October 1973 (US), b/w 'Son and Daughter'. Released as a single b-side, 14 October 1991, b/w 'The Show Must Go On'.

Queen's sturdy first single displays the hallmarks of the classic Queen sound: Mercury's exuberant vocals, May's multi-tracked, effects-laden guitars, Taylor's pounding drums, the stacked vocal harmonies. 'Keep Yourself Alive' was written during the short tenure of bassist Barry Michell (August 1970 to January 1971).

May's heavily phased and echoed guitars open the track and the arrangement builds with instruments entering in turn: 2nd guitar, lead guitar, high-hat, drums and bass, vocals. This was a trick used to great effect in 'Day Tripper' and 'Smoke on the Water'. Both may well have looked back to the awesome 'Tequila' by the Champs, released in 1958.

Freddie's heavily echoed vocals overlap through the verses and are double-tracked at the end of the second chorus. Queen's trademark harmonies ring through. There's even a drum solo. How very 1973.

The chorus is very commercial, but the song is less high-spirited in the verses and bridge and does take a while to get going. This imbalance is perhaps why 'Keep Yourself Alive' didn't trouble the charts. More and better was to come, but here was a band, and a singer, that thoroughly demanded attention.

'Keep Yourself Alive' was part of Queen's set from the very early days, and was performed throughout the 1970s, through to the conclusion of their tour to promote *The Game*, which ended in November 1981. On the 1980 and 1981 tours, the song would begin with a full-band improvisation jam and segue into Taylor's drum solo. 'Keep Yourself Alive' was performed as part of a medley of older songs in 1984, and, to great effect, with Adam Lambert.

The 2011 release of *Queen* includes the band's original demo of 'Keep Yourself Alive', recorded in December 1971, several months before the formal sessions for *Queen*. This is taken from Brian May's own acetate.

'My favourite gem,' he says, 'is the original acetate which has on it all the demos we made prior to signing with Trident in the very beginning. Nobody has ever heard these recordings before – I think I'm the owner of the only acetate in the world! It includes a version of 'Keep Yourself Alive' which is something very special. You're hearing Queen before anybody touched us or tried to mould us. [6]

The song was recorded twice for the BBC: on 5 February 1973 and 25 July 1973. Both have been released on *On Air*.

'Keep Yourself Alive' was re-recorded in June 1975 during sessions for *A Night of the Opera*. The 1975 version was planned as a US-only single but was shelved and remained unheard until 2011 when it was included on a re-issue of *A Night of the Opera*. It sounds very much like the 1972 version but with a fuller sound – more guitars here and there and added punctuations in the drum arrangement.

'Doing All Right' (Brian May / Tim Staffell)

A song from the Smile days, written by Brian May and Smile bassist Tim Staffell. It was recorded by Smile in June 1969 at Trident Studios. In the Queen version, a song of two halves, May plays acoustic guitar and piano before a loud rock section takes the listener by surprise.

The arrangement is fussy and too clever by half, but it's very progressive for 1969. Almost fifty years on this song still sounds fresh and new: Mercury sings it with real conviction. The combination of a slow ballad section and a loud rock interlude was a technique revisited in 'The March of the Black Queen' and perfected in 'Bohemian Rhapsody'.

'Doing All Right' was added to Queen's set in 1974 and was performed regularly until summer 1976. The song was recorded 5 February 1973, London, for the BBC and released on *Live at the Beeb*, the 'Let Me Live' CD single, and on *On Air*.

'Great King Rat' (Freddie Mercury)

Freddie Mercury's first song for Queen, if you listen to the albums in order, is 'Great King Rat'. It is quintessential early Queen: a dense, lithe composition with many changes in metre. Although mostly in 4/4, 'Great King Rat' has occasional measures of 5/4 and 7/4. There is also a long Led Zeppelin-inspired guitar solo.

From the beginning, Mercury's songs were unlike anyone else's – a unique combination of progressive rock, glam rock, fantasy and pop. 'Great King Rat' was written on guitar, mostly in A minor. Mercury's inexperience on the instrument gives the basis of the song an appealing simplicity. Mercury's Queen bandmates, right from the first album, were able to stamp their sound and add their style onto songs such as 'Great King Rat' – no-one else sounded like Queen in 1973. It took listeners a while to catch up.

'Great King Rat' was performed in 1973 and during the first half of 1974, promoting *Queen* and *Queen II*. The De Lane Lea demo, recorded December 1971, has been released on the 2011 re-issue of *Queen*. Two versions were recorded for the BBC: 5 February 1973 and 3 December 1973 both on *On Air*.

'My Fairy King' (Freddie Mercury)
'My Fairy King' is set in Rhye, a fantasy world created by Freddie Mercury and featured, notably, in 'Seven Seas of Rhye'. One of the songs that builds on the Led Zeppelin template but adds elements of progressive rock, 'My Fairy King' has nonsense lyrics, splashes of vocal harmonies, a harmonic multi-track guitar introduction that foreshadows 'Brighton Rock', Freddie's distinctive percussive piano sound and shifting sections including an exciting guitar-led ending which resolves to a slow, bluesy finale. Its inventive sound palette and complex structure point towards 'The March of the Black Queen' and 'Bohemian Rhapsody'.

The line 'Mother Mercury, look what they've done to me' is said to have trigged Freddie Bulsara to permanently adopt a new name.

'My Fairy King' is known to have been performed in concert by Queen only a very few times, always as a tease or on-the-spot improvisation by Freddie Mercury: once in 1982, three times in 1984 during a run of gigs in Sun City and once in Japan in 1985.

'My Fairy King' was also recorded for the BBC on 5 February 1973 and released on *Live at the Beeb*, on the 'Let Me Live' CD single, and on *On Air*.

'Liar' (Freddie Mercury)
Released a single a-side, 11 February 1974 (US), b/w 'Doing All Right'.

Although credited to Freddie Mercury, 'Liar', an important early song, was based on a riff from an old Ibex song called 'Lover', re-worked by Brian May with lyrics by Mercury. 'Liar' is experimentation from start to finish: the obligatory heavy riffs alternate with folky verses, a call-and-answer vocal section and a pop-rock chorus. Led Zeppelin's 'Ramble On' meets Steeleye Span meets Argent. There was certainly no lack of self-confidence in Queen.

'Liar' was Queen's regular set-closer until 1974 and stayed in the set until the end of 1977.

The De Lane Lea demo, recorded December 1971, was released on the 2011 re-issue of *Queen*. A US single chops up the song with many edits to just under three minutes in length. A remix released on the 1991 re-issue of *Queen* has louder percussion. An edited version, just the introduction, was released as part of *The eYe* video game. Also recorded twice for BBC: 5 February 1973 released on *Live at the Beeb*, on the 'Let Me Live' CD single, and on *On Air*; 25 July 1973, released on *On Air*.

'The Night Comes Down' (Brian May)

When Queen went into Trident Studios to record their debut album in summer 1972, they recorded a version of this Brian May song, one of the first he wrote for Queen. A full version was completed, but the band thought that they hadn't improved on their original demo from late the previous year. The demo version was used on the finished album, and the 1972 version remains unheard.

The first two Queen albums build the foundations of the sound that would make Queen great – Freddie Mercury's soaring vocals, Brian May's multiple guitar work and songs that are as a curious mixture of heavy metal, prog rock, glam and a masterful pop touch. 'The Night Comes Down' is an early indication of the kind of epic operatic rock that would become Queen's signature sound in the second half of the 1970s.

There is a nod to The Beatles in the lyric: 'When I was young it came to me / And I could see the sun breaking / Lucy was high and so was I'. There is a touch of 1967 phasing on the drums at this point in the song.

With complex time signatures, closely-miked acoustic guitars and drums, and a gorgeous Freddie vocal showing his full range, 'The Night Comes Down' stands out amongst a debut album laden with pop-tinged glam/metal: this is a song with real substance. The confidence is growing, but in 'The Night Comes Down' there is a still a sensitivity that was sometimes lost in their later work.

There is only one confirmed live performance: in London in March 1972. No doubt the song was performed at other concerts around this period.

The De Lane Lea demo, recorded December 1971, was released on the 2011 re-issue of *Queen*. This is the same recording as we hear on *Queen*, but with a different drier mix – the drums especially are less up-front. An edited version, just the introduction, was released as part of *The eYe* video game.

'Modern Times Rock 'n' Roll' (Roger Taylor)

Roger Taylor's songs always provided a change of pace within a Queen album. 'Modern Times Rock 'n' Roll' is a fast blues with a churning guitar riff, driving rhythm section, pumping piano and a typically powerful lead vocal from Taylor. Think of Led Zeppelin's 'Rock and Roll' or 'Communication Breakdown' on helium. It's very fast and very short.

'Modern Times Rock 'n' Roll' was performed on occasion in 1973, then a set regular until mid-1975, usually as part of the encore, with infrequent outings through mid-1976.

'Modern Times Rock 'n' Roll' was recorded at three of the band's BBC sessions: 5 February 1973, 3 December 1973 and 3 April 1974. These are all on *On Air*. There is also an instrumental version released as part of The *eYe* video game.

'Son and Daughter' (Brian May)

Released as a single b-side, 6 July 1973, b/w 'Keep Yourself Alive'.

'Son and Daughter', written around May's catchy guitar riff – borrowed from Led Zeppelin's 'Heartbreaker' – is typical of the blues rock that Queen performed in the early days. Its lumbering pace, syncopated bass/guitar riffs and Freddie's low-range, almost distorted, vocals suggest Black Sabbath crossed with the Beatles' 'Come Together' – only bursts of harmony backing vocals and those Brian May guitar squalls lift this above almost generic heavy metal.

'Son and Daughter' was performed in concert from the earliest concerts (at a much faster tempo) through to the end of the *A Night at the Opera* tour in April 1976. Only one verse was performed from November 1975 onwards. Three versions of 'Son and Daughter' were recorded for the BBC: on 5 February 1973, 25 July 1973 and 3 December 1973. All were released on *On Air* in 2016. Early performances include an embryonic version of the guitar solo later to grace 'Brighton Rock'.

'Jesus' (Freddie Mercury)

'Jesus' is a psychedelic rock song, laden with May's heavily-treated guitars, a very clear and powerful lead vocal and somewhat corny and overstated lyrics.

'Packed with enough religious fervour to bore a Pope,' suggests Martin Power in *The Complete Guide to the Music of Queen*.

Or, as Mark Blake suggests, 'The fervent 'Jesus' [is] an early example of Mercury's lyrical ambition: like a Cecil B. De Mille biblical epic condensed into three and a half minutes, or Freddie's art A-Level crucifixion painting set to music.'

The long instrumental break perhaps takes the song beyond its natural conclusion. The song is known to have been performed by Queen only on two occasions, both in 1972. The De Lane Lea demo, recorded December 1971, was released on the 2011 re-issue of *Queen*.

'Seven Seas of Rhye' (instrumental version) (Freddie Mercury)

An instrumental teaser, slower than the remake for *Queen II*. They were right to wait until the song was ready as the full version would be their first hit single.

'There is a little fragment on our first album,' says Brian May. 'Freddie has this idea, but it wasn't developed, so we just put down what we had. We [later] thought that it would be a good basis for a single.'[7]

Other contemporary songs

'Polar Bear'

A slow, bluesy Smile song recorded by them in September 1969. The song was also performed by Queen in their early sets and was recorded for *Queen* in 1972; a high-quality studio outtake exists but Freddie's heart isn't really in it.

'Feelings'
A demo of this song is known to exist – it's an early version of 'Feelings, Feelings' which the band would record in 1977 but not release until 2017.

'Silver Salmon'
Another Smile song, possibly written by Tim Staffell and recorded by Queen as a demo in 1972 but not taken further.

'Hangman'
An early Freddie Mercury original, sub-Black Sabbath heavy metal. It probably dates from the Ibex / Wreckage days but was certainly performed by Queen in their earliest concerts and occasionally as late as 1976. Several in-concert recordings have surfaced over the years: two of these have been officially released as part of the band's Top 100 Bootlegs project recorded at Colston Hall, Bristol on 29 November 1973 and the Budokan Hall, Tokyo, Japan on 1 May 1975. It has never officially been taken into the studio, but a private collector has claimed that he owns an acetate of a studio recording. If so, he's hanging onto it.

'Hangman … was very much based on Free,' Roger Taylor told *Q* magazine in 2005. 'It had that spare blues riff thing that was very much Free's forte.'

'Mad the Swine'
'Mad the Swine' dates from the early sessions for the album and was planned as the fourth track on *Queen*, between 'Great King Rat' and 'My Fairy King'. The arrangement suggests that the song was composed on guitar. The song was first released in May 1991 on a CD single with 'Headlong' and 'All God's People', and later on the 2011 re-issue of *Queen*.

'Rock and Roll medley'
A reliable encore from the earliest concerts, right through the '70s. 'Jailhouse Rock' was a regular, along with 'Shake, Rattle and Roll', 'Stupid Cupid', 'Be-Bop-A-Lula' and 'Lucille' and others. A studio version is rumoured to exist. In later years, the medley would provide a change of pace within the set. A version of this was released on *Live at Wembley '86*, consisting of '(You're So Square) Baby I Don't Care', 'Hello Mary Lou (Goodbye Heart)', 'Tutti Frutti' and 'Gimme Some Lovin''.

'I Can Hear Music', 'Goin' Back'
The a-side and b-side of a 1973 single credited to Larry Lurex, recorded during sessions for *Queen*. Three out of the four members of Queen took part (Mercury, May and Taylor).

Queen II (1973)

Personnel:
Freddie Mercury: lead vocals, backing vocals, piano, harpsichord
Brian May: electric guitar, acoustic guitar, lead vocals, backing vocals, bells, piano
Roger Taylor (credited as 'Roger Meddows-Taylor'): drums, backing vocals, lead vocals, gong, marimba, percussion
John Deacon: bass, acoustic guitar
+ Roy Thomas Baker: castanets on 'The Fairy Feller's Master Stroke', stylophone on 'Seven Seas of Rhye'.
Recorded in August 1973 at Trident Studios, London. Produced by Roy Thomas Baker, Geoffrey Cable and Queen.
UK released date: 8 March 1974. US release date: 9 April 1974.
Highest chart places: UK: 5, US: 49.

The title of *Queen II* is appropriate as the band's second album is very much a sequel to, or an extension of, their first. It also, perhaps subconsciously, follows Led Zeppelin, whose second album, the similarly titled *Led Zeppelin II*, included 'Whole Lotta Love' (see 'Get Down, Make Love') and 'Heartbreaker' (see 'Son and Daughter').

The name, though, is the only prosaic element of this album.

In *Queen II* we start to hear the band's sound coalesce into three styles: the rocker ('Seven Seas of Rhye', 'Ogre Battle'), the ballad ('Some Day, One Day', 'White Queen (As It Began)', 'Nevermore') and the anthem ('Father to Son', 'Funny How Love Is', 'Procession', 'The March of the Black Queen'). At least three songs date from the *Queen* period ('Father to Son', 'Ogre Battle', 'Seven Seas of Rhye') and one from Smile ('White Queen (As It Began)').

'Where its predecessor was a hotchpotch of proto-metal bombast and fey mysticism, *Queen II* was bold and tremendously ambitious,' wrote Dave Everley in 2005. 'The kitchen sink hasn't quite been uprooted, but the cutlery drawer was definitely in the mix.'

May wrote most of the music for the album's Side White: presented as the first half of the album on CD reissues and downloads. The stately guitar prelude 'Procession' leads directly into 'Father to Son'.

Freddie's contributions to the album, including the quintuple whammy of the powerful, frenetic 'Ogre Battle', the blithe 'The Fairy Feller's Master-Stroke' – a dry run for the kind of music-hall rock they'd perfect with the next album's 'Killer Queen' – the gorgeous, plaintive 'Nevermore', the majestic *magnum opus* 'The March of the Black Queen', and the Beach Boys-influenced 'Funny How Love Is'. These five songs run as single piece of music through seventeen minutes of Side Black, with the scintillating 'Seven Seas of Rhye' as a coda.

'It just evolved to where there was a batch of songs that could be considered aggressive,' Freddie told *Sounds* in 1976. 'A Black Side. And there was the smoother side.'

These seventeen minutes established Mercury as a writer and musician of rare talent – subsequent live shows confirmed his unparalleled skills as a frontman.

The album was recorded at Trident Studios, without limitations on studio time or hours. Elton John had mixed *Goodbye Yellow Brick Road* at Trident just before Queen started work on *Queen II*.

'Despite the complexity and sophistication of *Queen II*,' writes Phil Chapman, 'it was recorded in about a month, a testament to the band's focus and work-rate.'

'The most important thing to me was the *Queen II* album going into the charts,' said John Deacon the following year, 'especially satisfying, since the first one didn't do so well. It's nice to see some recognition for your work.' [8]

'Procession' (Brian May)

A multi-guitar anthem – the opening heartbeat suggests the influence of Pink Floyd's *The Dark Side of the Moon*, released six months before *Queen II* was recorded.

'Procession' was performed as the opening song on all live dates from 1973 to 1977. It was replaced by the opening intro to *A Day at the Races* for the second half of the *A Day at the Races* tour. A recording of the piece was used to open all of the concerts on the first two legs of the Queen + Adam Lambert tour in 2014, segueing into 'Now I'm Here'.

'Father to Son' (Brian May)

Utterly bombastic but with a tender message beneath, 'Father to Son' is a powerful, anthemic hard rock/progressive power ballad. It's a kind of son of 'Liar' with hints of the Who and the Rolling Stones. 'Father to Son' has a typically grand production – layers of guitars and vocals – and a lyric that will resonate with men of a certain age who are recognising that they are turning into their fathers: 'A word in your ear from father to son / Funny you don't hear a single word I say.'

As Oscar Wilde said, 'All women become like their mothers. That is their tragedy. No man does, and that is his.'

'Father to Son' was performed live as the set-opener from September 1973 to May 1974, and regularly until 1976.

'White Queen (As It Began)' (Brian May)

Released on *Queen's First EP*, 20 May 1977. UK 17.

The genesis of this song pre-dates the formation of Queen: it was written, or at least started, in 1969 during the Smile era. It's pure early Queen and one of Brian May's best songs. Essentially 'White Queen (As It Began)' is a fragile prog rock ballad with a powerful, energetic conclusion. The usual wonderful lead vocal, impeccable harmonies, intelligent lyrics, building tension and shifting dynamics are all in place.

'White Queen (As It Began)' was performed live from 1974 to 1978. 'White

Queen (As It Began)' was recorded for the BBC on 3 April 1974. This version can be heard on *On Air*. The song had a revised, surely definitive, arrangement in 1975, with a new piano part and a beautifully controlled echoed, extended guitar solo from Brian May. Listen to *A Night at the Odeon – Hammersmith '75* and witness Queen at full power, on the brink of global success.

'Some Day One Day' (Brian May)

A simple (for Queen) folk-influenced song, with a Brian May lead vocal and some delicious, spiralling guitar harmonies.

'The Loser in the End' (Roger Taylor)

After giving us a Led Zeppelin pastiche on *Queen*, Taylor apes *Deep Purple in Rock* with a touch of 'Sparks' by The Who in the riff. Mercury wisely steers clear.

'Ogre Battle' (Freddie Mercury)

This ferocious song starts with phased white noise, some nifty reversed sound effects (the end of the song played backwards) and a furious guitar riff. 'Ogre Battle' is epic, energetic, fast and loud: proto heavy metal *a la* early Rush.

"Ogre Battle' [has] a very heavy metal guitar riff,' noted Brian May in 1998. 'It's strange that Freddie should have done that. But when he used to pick up a guitar he'd have a great frenetic energy. It was kind of like a very nervy animal playing the guitar. He was a very impatient person and was very impatient with his own technique. He didn't have a great technical ability on the guitar but had it in his head. And you could feel this stuff bursting to get out.' [9]

'Ogre Battle' was performed in concert from 1973 to 1977. Versions for the BBC recorded 5 February 1973 (the first recorded version of this song) and 3 December 1973 are available on *On Air*.

A remix released on the 1991 re-issue of *Queen II* has some different guitar effects and added drums. A version with a clean ending (the gong fades naturally rather than cutting to the opening of 'The Fairy Feller's Master-Stroke') is on *Deep Cuts, Volume 1*, released in 2011.

'The Fairy Feller's Master-Stroke' (Freddie Mercury)

'The Fairy Feller's Master-Stroke' was named after a painting by Richard Dadd which is in the Tate Gallery in London. The song points towards 'Bohemian Rhapsody' in its form and complexity.

A busy and rhythmically complex introduction leads to an opening vocal section, some in falsetto, then a 'verse' section with a silly interlude (1:18-1:45) featuring harpsichord and electric guitar. John Deacon's bass playing here is very strong and holds the song together as it threatens to come off the rails entirely. A bridge section ('soldier sailor tinker tailor ploughboy') leads back to the verse. No-one else would write lyrics such as these in 1973: 'Oberon and

Titania watched by a harridan / Mab is the queen and there's a good apothecary man'. Perhaps for good reason. The piano-led conclusion leads directly into 'Nevermore'.

Performed occasionally in 1974.

'Nevermore' (Freddie Mercury)

'Nevermore' is Queen's first piano/vocal ballad – there are no guitars. It sets up the album's central epic 'The March of the Black Queen'. It's pure Freddie: heartfelt, focussed, beautifully sung.

Though never performed live, 'Nevermore' was recorded for the BBC on 3 April 1974. This version was released on the 2011 reissue of *Queen II*, and as part of *On Air* (released in 2016).

'The March of The Black Queen' (Freddie Mercury)

The grandiose, magnificent, valiant 'The March of The Black Queen' might be an utterly ludicrous song, but it's one of Queen's best. The innovation and invention almost pull the song apart. But, somehow, the band's skill holds it all together.

"The March of the Black Queen', that took ages. I had to give it everything, to be self-indulgent or whatever'. Freddie Mercury interview with Caroline Coon, *Melody Maker*, December 1974.

'The March of the Black Queen' is a favourite of progressive rock fans. It has many different non-repeating sections: almost a suite of separate songs.

0:00   The song starts with slow, dramatic piano chords and guitar trills.

0:20   Section 1 – pulsing bass, sustained backing vocals and the repetition of double-tracked Freddie immediately questioning 'do you mean it?' Is it a co-incidence both this song and 'Bohemian Rhapsody' open with a question? Throughout 'The March of the Black Queen' it is the backing vocals that provide the underlying chords for the arrangement. The descending guitar line at 0:37 would be re-used in 'nothing really matters' in 'Bohemian Rhapsody'.

0:42   The arrangement moves to double-time with piano, tom-toms and spiralling vocal harmonies which reappear in the 'magnifico' section of 'Bohemian Rhapsody'.

1:05   Section 2 – the arrangement simplifies (a little) for this 'verse' section. Freddie sings 'You've never seen nothing like it, no never in your life / Like going up to heaven and then coming back alive'. Subsequent vocal lines overlap and push to each side of the stereo spectrum, as with 'Keep Yourself Alive'. Freddie's trademark bar-room piano is juxtaposed with bass guitar.

1:21   The chorus, of sorts. 'Here comes the Black Queen, poking in the pile / Fie-fo the black Queen, marching single file'.

1:38   May's first, brief guitar break repeating some of the themes from the previous 'coming back alive' and 'lily pool delight' sections two subsections before.

1:47 A second 'verse' and 'chorus' section.

2:10 A second guitar break, this time with the wah-wah pedal later a feature of the rock section of 'Bohemian Rhapsody'. Indeed, this whole section – tempo, arrangement – sounds a lot like Queen's classic 1975 song.

2:24 Another abrupt change, into 12/8 time and two unrelated lead guitar parts, then what sounds like tubular bells, and ascending polyrhythmic vocal harmonies against descending piano. [10]

3:00 Section 3 – another abrupt change in tempo brings us back to the piano ballad format. But this is a new composition, not repeated from earlier sections of the song. Here we have the essence of Freddie Mercury with his multitracked vocals, expressive piano, odd time measures and uplifting lyrics: 'In each and every soul lies a man, very soon he'll deceive and discover / but even till the end of his life, he'll bring a little love'.

4:02 A linking section with vocal harmonies and lively bass guitar and a key change to take us into part 4.

4:20 Section 4 – a new key and a new tempo, rockier in feel, but not heavy. Some of the melody and lyrics link back to the 'verse' section, but are not the same as previous sections, especially the repeats of the title phrase.

4:54 The lead and bass guitars both hold a note until the flowering of the guitar solo, similar to the first at 1:38. More harmony vocals and a repeat of the 'black queen' melody.

5:38 Another change of pace for a section then is a definite precursor to the 'any way the wind blows' in 'Bohemian Rhapsody' – the feel is identical.

6:08 A coda, with an unexpected return to the melody from the 'verse' section takes us directly into 'Funny How Love Is'.

A remix with a clean ending (no cross fade, just a deeply echoed vocal harmony) is on *Deep Cuts, Volume 1*, released in 2011.

Parts of 'The March of the Black Queen' were performed live from October 1974 to September 1976. The song was too complex to be performed in full, but the up-tempo section four containing the lines 'My life is in your hands / I'll foe and I'll fie...' was often included in a medley with 'Killer Queen'.

'Funny How Love Is' (Freddie Mercury)

A studio composition, reminiscent of 'I Can Hear Music' by the Beach Boys, or even late period Abba. The vocal harmonies, wall-of-sound acoustic guitars and mixed-back rhythm section mark this out as an unusual song in the Queen catalogue. 'Funny How Love Is' segues so carefully from 'The March of the Black Queen' that the two songs can almost be heard as one performance. The Japanese CD single version has a clean intro without the cross-fade from 'The March of the Black Queen'

'Seven Seas of Rhye' (Freddie Mercury)

Released as a single a-side, 23 February 1974 (UK) and 20 June 1974 (US), b/w 'See What a Fool I've Been'. UK: 10. Released on *Greatest Hits*, 26 October 1981. Released as a single b-side, 9 June 1986, b/w 'Friends Will Be Friends'. Queen's first hit, a top ten hit in the UK. [11]

'Seven Seas of Rhye' is a short, compact melange of the irresistible ingredients of early Queen: hammered piano intro in an odd time signature, pounding drums, guitar harmonies, bouncing bass line, stopped riffs, echo on everything, Roger Taylor's falsetto backing vocals and an unusually low, growling double-tracked vocal from Freddie Mercury.

Queen's hit single career was kick-started by a stroke of good fortune. The biggest pop show in the UK was *Top of the Pops*. With its high viewing figures every Thursday evening, *Top of the Pops* was a significant part of British culture in the 1960s, 1970s and 1980s – and audience viewing figures each week were huge.

Shortly after returning from a miserable visit to Australia the band was offered a last-minute replacement slot on *Top of the Pops* on 21 February 1974. Jumping at the opportunity they premiered 'Seven Seas of Rhye' from the as-yet-unreleased *Queen II*. The song was rush-released as a single two days later. Freddie Mercury would soon quit his day job working at a clothes stall at Kensington Market.

The closing sound effects of 'I Do Like to be Beside the Seaside' are revisited in 'Brighton Rock', the first song on their next album.

'Seven Seas of Rhye' was included in live concerts from March 1974 through to April 1976, then again from August 1984 to Freddie's final gig with Queen at Knebworth on 9 August 1986. Taylor and May performed 'Seven Seas of Rhye' with Midge Ure at the 2010 Prince's Trust concert, and with Adam Lambert on their tours together.

An instrumental remix is on the 2011 re-issue of *Queen II*. A dance remix with only a heavily echoed Freddie vocal track and the very occasional snatch of guitar from the original is on the 1991 re-issue of *Queen II*. A pulsing bass and a processed piano track move this remix towards 'Another One Bites the Dust', but even then, it sounds almost nothing like Queen. The remix also includes samples from other Queen songs such as 'Crazy Little Thing Called Love', 'Mustapha', 'White Man' and others.

Other contemporary songs
'See What a Fool I've Been'

The B-side of 'Seven Seas of Rhye', released 23 February 1974. Available on the 1991 and 2011 re-issues of *Queen II*. This slow blues-rocker pre-dates the formation of Queen: it was written in early 1969 during the Smile era and performed by them from time to time. 'See What a Fool I've Been' was also sung live by Queen on occasion in 1973, 1974 and 1975. It's a rewrite of 'That's How I Feel' by American blues musician Sonny Terry.

'See What a Fool I've Been' was recorded for the BBC on 25 July 1973 and released on both the 2011 re-issue of *Queen II* and on *On Air* (2016).

'Fly by Night'
A John Deacon song presumed written around this time.

'Deep Ridge'
A Brian May song presumed written around this time.

Sheer Heart Attack (1974)

Personnel:
Freddie Mercury: lead vocals, backing vocals, piano, organ
Brian May: electric guitar, acoustic guitar, backing vocals, lead vocals, piano, banjolele
Roger Taylor: drums, percussion, backing vocals, lead vocals
John Deacon: bass guitar, electric guitar, acoustic guitar, double bass.
Recorded mid to late July 1974 at Rockfield, Wales; early to late August 1974 at Wessex Sound Studio, London; mid-August 1974 at AIR, London; September 1974 at Trident, London. Produced by Roy Thomas Baker and Queen.
UK release date: 8 November 1974. US release date: 12 November 1974.
Highest chart places: UK: 2, USA: 12.

Sheer Heart Attack was Queen's commercial breakthrough and first masterpiece, but not without suffering. Brian May developed hepatitis during the band's first tour of the US and collapsed in New York on 12 May 1974 after a six-night run at the Uris Theatre on Broadway.
   'I felt like my whole body was made of lead,' said May later. 'I dragged myself to the bathroom and saw that I was a deep shade of yellow. That was the end of us conquering America at one shake. They smuggled me onto the plane back to England where I was ordered to bed for six weeks.' [12]
   May's enforced recovery meant that he missed many of the early sessions for *Sheer Heart Attack*. A relapse later that summer necessitated further nonappearances. In his absence, his bandmates wrote and recorded many songs of their own. Freddie Mercury broadened Queen's sound to include baroque balladry ('Lily of the Valley', 'In the Lap of the Gods … Revisited'), music hall pastiche ('Bring Back That Leroy Brown'), arch nastiness ('Flick of the Wrist') and a terrific piano-led bubble-gum-pop hit single ('Killer Queen'). Taylor gave us the classic glam-rock of 'Tenement Funster', and Deacon played guitar on four songs, including his own 'Misfire'. May's return added the powerful ('Brighton Rock'), the poetic ('Dear Friends') and the song performed more than any another ('Now I'm Here'). The piano/guitar/bass/drums instrumentation was embellished by double bass and ukulele-banjo ('Bring

Back That Leroy Brown'), Hammond organ ('Now I'm Here') and jangle piano ('Killer Queen'). It wasn't by chance that *Sheer Heart Attack* has a commercial sheen, both in production and melody, lacking in *Queen* and *Queen II*.

Jac Holzman: 'I had seen artists make wonderful albums but because they didn't have momentum the public didn't give them the time necessary [to progress]. Queen had momentum'. [13]

Like *Queen II*, the front cover image was photographed by Mick Rock. The distinctive 'sweaty' look was achieved by smearing the band in Vaseline and then spraying them with water. John Deacon looks decidedly unimpressed.

The album is very varied, we took it to extremes I suppose, but we are very interested in studio techniques and wanted to use what was available. We learnt a lot about technique while we were making the first two albums. Of course, there has been some criticism, and the constructive criticism has been very good for us. But to be frank I'm not that keen on the British music press, and they've been pretty unfair to us. I think we're good writers – and we want to play good music, no matter how much of a slagging we get. The music is the most important factor.
Freddie Mercury, *Melody Maker*, November 1974

'Brighton Rock' (Brian May)

Written in 1973, but held back, 'Brighton Rock' exists for one reason: to showcase Brian May's considerable skills as a guitarist. For over three minutes, longer than any of the songs on the first *seven* Beatles albums, May delivers that legendary solo, parts of which can be traced to a song called 'Blag', recorded with Smile in September 1969 and to many live versions of 'Son and Daughter'. The concert versions are lengthier still: the longest ever version is around fifteen minutes and includes a timpani solo by Roger Taylor.

'Brighton Rock' opens with fairground music, suggesting the 'happy little day' at the seaside. The first verses are sung mostly in falsetto before swooping down for the 'oh, rock of ages' section. For the astonishing solo – more remarkable as May had been hospitalised not long before – the other instrumentalists drop out completely. From around 3:30 May uses an Echoplex tape delay effect which allows him to harmonise and duet with himself. The powerful rhythm section re-enters and the band play a final verse and the song ends on a Jimi Hendrix chord.

The multitracks confirm that even more guitars were recorded but not used in the final mix: no fewer than twelve guitar tracks – some dry, some echoes, power chords, rhythm chording at the nut, fills when capoed higher up the neck, lead under 2nd verse, solo section, Echoplexed solo section ... all of these were mixed out for *Sheer Heart Attack*.

'Brighton Rock' was performed live, in full, from November 1975 to May 1979. For the tours promoting *The Game* (1980-1981) and *The Works* (1984-1985), Brian May would end his solo guitar part of the show with the end section of 'Brighton Rock' and the band would return to perform the final verse.

An edited version, just the introduction, was released as part of *The eYe* video game.

'Killer Queen' (Freddie Mercury)

Released as a single a-side, 11 October 1974, b/w 'Flick of the Wrist'. UK: 2. US: 12. Released on *Greatest Hits*, 1981.

A wonderfully commercial song, and yet effortlessly clever and complex in execution, 'Killer Queen' was surely a conscious move away from the prog-glam of *Queen* and *Queen II*. It was a major UK hit, only held off Number One by David Essex' 'I'm Gonna Make You a Star'.

'Most people hearing this for the first time really were shocked,' says Brian May, 'because it wasn't rock, like they expected us to be – it was very sophisticated, very delicate. It's a beautifully crafted record and totally Freddie. I love it.' [14]

Freddie in 1974:

Well, Killer Queen I wrote in one night. I'm not being conceited or anything, but it just fell into place. Certain songs do ... I scribbled down the words in the dark one Saturday night and the next morning I got them all together and I worked all day Sunday and that was it. I'd got it. It gelled. It was great. 'Killer Queen' was one song which was really out of the format that I usually write in. Usually the music comes first, but the words came to me, and the sophisticated style that I wanted to put across in the song, came first. Certain things just come together, but other things you have to work for.' [15]

Mostly recorded without May, 'Killer Queen' includes the first flowering of the multi-tracking and vocal harmonising methods that would go on to become big parts of Queen's signature sound.

May's main contribution is a guitar solo that elaborates on the vocal melody of the verses.

0:00   A simple finger-clicking introduction leads straight into the first verse with its vivid lyrical imagery. On the master-tapes Taylor can be heard counting in, so these finger clicks are an overdub. They last right through to the words 'Marie Antionette'. The piano here and throughout is double-tracked. The master tapes reveal that a grand piano was used for the basic take – with bass and drums – and that the upright tack piano was added later.

0:22   A short link section ('caviar and cigarettes / well versed in etiquette / extraordinarily nice') signals the first chorus, which is asymmetrical ending with the classic harmonised and phased 'guaranteed to blow your mind … any time!'.

0:37   A repeat of the link section ('recommended at the price / insatiable an appetite / wanna try?') with some fabulous guitar/piano interaction.

0:52   The second verse has cunning 'conversation/complication' and 'address/ baroness' rhymes and some gorgeous harmonised backing vocals. There are plenty of on-line conspiracy theories about the true meaning of the phrase 'Geisha Minah' used in this verse.

1:09   A link section with another rich and colourful lyric in the next link section ('fastidious and precise'). One of the tracks on the master tape is used solely for John Deacon's descending bass run here.

1:15   A second chorus.

1:25   Brian May's juicy solo plays off against the piano, triple-tracked in places, very symphonic in approach and execution. "Killer Queen' has the guitar solo I'd most like to be remembered for,' May commented in 2009. [16]

2:02   An irregular bridge section ('drop of a hat …'), and a third chorus, with thicker vocal and guitar harmonies.

2:27   An unexpected revisit of the link section ('recommended at the price') with phased harmonies on 'wanna try?'

2:40   The song ends with a carefully arranged finale based on a series of double-stops with a repeating stereo-effect guitar figure, carefully overdubbed, to fade.

'Killer Queen' proved that Queen could write songs that were simultaneously complex and commercial. In this respect, it's one of the most important songs in the Queen catalogue. The road to 'Bohemian Rhapsody' was now clearly defined.

'Killer Queen' was a set regular from 1974 to 1981, and again in 1984-1985, always truncated and often as part of a medley – the third verse was never performed live. It was also performed with both Paul Rodgers and Adam Lambert.

Freddie Mercury would be awarded his first Ivor Novello award for 'Killer Queen' on 22 May 1975. 'It's about a high-class call girl,' he told *New Musical Express* in November 1974. 'I'm trying to say that classy people can be whores as well. That's what the song is about, though I'd prefer people to put their interpretation upon it – to read into it what they like.

'Tenement Funster' (Roger Taylor)

'Tenement Funster' is the first of three songs on side one of *Sheer Heart Attack* that run continuously as a single piece of music. It is Roger Taylor's first classic song, featuring John Deacon on acoustic guitar, Freddie Mercury on piano, some heavy electric guitar from Brian May and layers of Taylor's lead and backing vocals. The same chords repeat through the verses, choruses and bridge, although they are beefed up with some powerful guitar chords in the chorus. The opening arpeggios (in Em and Am) appear in two of Taylor's songs from 1977 – 'Rock It (Prime Jive)' and 'Human Body' (the b-side of 'Play the Game'). The subject matter is a politically incorrect nod to Taylor's love of the rock and roll lifestyle and the benefits it brings. It sounds like Free crossed with Black Sabbath.

The single version, released on *Queen's First EP* 20 May 1977 (UK 17) ends with a final guitar chord and some feedback, rather than immediately cross-fading to 'Flick of the Wrist'. 'Tenement Funster' was also recorded for the BBC on 16 October 1974 and released on *On Air* in 2016.

'Flick of the Wrist' (Freddie Mercury)
Released as a single b-side, 11 October 1974 (UK and US), b/w 'Killer Queen'. UK: 2. US: 12.

A brilliantly bitter, aggressively nasty, churningly chilling tune with Queen's patent tuneful heavy metal and multi-part vocals. Is this a precursor to 'Death on Two Legs'? 'Prostitute yourself he says / Castrate your human pride / Sacrifice your leisure days / Let me squeeze you till you've dried'.

The complex central section features one of Brian May's most unhinged guitar solos. And, this being Queen, there is a sing-a-long chorus disguising those harsh lyrics. The song was performed live from 1974 to 1976.

The single edit starts with a clean piano intro: there is no cross-fade from 'Tenement Funster' as heard on the album; it ends with a burst of (reversed?) feedback and doesn't cross-fade immediately into 'Lily of the Valley'. Also recorded for the BBC on 16 October 1974 and released on *On Air* in 2016.

'Lily of the Valley' (Freddie Mercury)
A beautiful, lyrical almost-perfect song with much of the pomp held in check. The key hook is the leaping piano motif in the introduction, then a swoop to a gorgeous, rich, genuine Freddie vocal backed by layers and layers of backing vocals. The climax at 'messenger from seven seas' is as gorgeous a piece of music as anything this band produced. This is a precursor to 'Love of My Life' and may well have been written for the same subject: Freddie's girlfriend Mary Austin. And, at less than two minutes in length, we are left wanting more. Simply sublime.

Released as a single b-side, 17 January 1975 (UK and US), b/w 'Now I'm Here'. This version starts cleanly with the opening piano flourish and is not cross-faded from 'Flick of the Wrist'.

'Now I'm Here' (Brian May)
Released as a single a-side, 17 January 1975 (UK and US), b/w 'Lily of the Valley'. UK: 11. Released on *Greatest Hits,* 1981. Released on the UK CD single for 'The Show Must Go On', 14 October 1991. Live version, recorded

at Festhalle Frankfurt, 2 February 1979, released as a single b-side, 19 June 1979. UK 63.

'Now I'm Here' is a straight-forward rocker, but with typical Queen twists. '[It] was started and finished in the last couple of weeks [of sessions for the album],' May wrote in *As It Began* in 1992, 'I'd finally got my ideas straight for the song while in hospital, reflecting on the future.'

May recalls events on Queen's US tour in April-May 1974 with Mott the Hoople ('Down in the city just Hoople 'n' me'), in particular a liaison in New Orleans with a girl called Peaches.'Whatever came of you and me / America's new bride to be / Down in the dungeon just Peaches 'n' me / Don't I love her so'

'Now I'm Here' starts with a strong, tight, tense power chord, with Freddie's rich tenor ('here I stand') leaping up to a startling falsetto ('look around, around, around'), punctuated by rhythm guitar, cymbals and bass drum. The tension builds through the 'just a new man' section and is released on the line 'and you made me live again' as May's heavily distorted guitar growls through short, punchy solo sections and the song careers into life.

A swirling organ sound and jaunty piano – both buried deep in the mix – enter at the 'don't I love him so' section before the guitar solo. The solo itself features lots of double stops – very Chuck Berry in style. The end section has another nod to Chuck Berry in the final line – 'go, go, go little queenie' is the chorus of Berry's 1959 hit of the same name.

'Now I'm Here 'was the first of many important single releases in mid-late January: 'Don't Stop Me Now' (26 January 1979), 'Save Me' (25 January 1980), 'Radio Ga Ga' (23 January 1984), 'Innuendo' (14 January 1991). It was recorded for the BBC on 3 April 1974 and released in 2016 on *On Air*. It was also recorded at the soundcheck for the December 1975 concert at Hammersmith Odeon and released as the b-side to 'Bohemian Rhapsody' (*A Night at the Odeon* version), in November 2015. 'Now I'm Here' is the Queen song performed in more concerts than any other – it was a permanent fixture in band's setlist for every tour from 1974 to 1986. It was also the opening song in concerts with Adam Lambert in 2014-2015.

'In the Lap of the Gods' (Freddie Mercury)

A startling progressive rock opening to what was side two of *Sheer Heart Attack* has Taylor's high falsetto, thrumming bass and tinkling piano arpeggios leading to a piano ballad verse with heavily processed lead vocals and fizzing percussion. It sounds like music from the end of the world. The verse resolves to a rich, melodic chorus ('leave it in the lap of the gods') with added acoustic guitar, a low, humming lead guitar and some more of those ball-busting falsettos. Beautiful. Other than Taylor's falsetto, the vocals are just Freddie Mercury, overdubbed many times.

The song was performed 1974-1975, starting at the verses: the introduction was never included in live performances.

'Stone Cold Crazy' (Queen)

Embryonic speed metal, written before *Queen II* but held back. Pulsing electric guitar and Taylor's hi-hat kick of the song, then we have that classic riff, which drops out for a mostly *a capella* verse with percussion and hi-hat, and two fast, furious and exciting guitar solos, the second with echoed harmonics. The song is powered by Taylor's drumming. It's all over in just over two minutes.

Performed live from 1974 to 1977, and again in 1984-1985. Also, part of Queen + Adam Lambert's tours in 2012-2013, 2016 and 2017. 'Stone Cold Crazy' was recorded for the BBC on 16 October 1974, released on *On Air*, 2016. There is a remix by Trent Reznor on the 1991 re-issue of *Sheer Heart Attack*. This is a full-on techno / heavy metal remix – exhausting but thrilling in equal measures. 'That should have been a good take!' comments Freddie, and he's not wrong.

'Dear Friends' (Brian May)

Also released on some versions of the *Five Live* EP (released 19 April 1993).

Just Freddie and Brian perform on this short, atmospheric piano ballad. It's a remarkable contrast to the preceding 'Stone Cold Crazy'. Mercury's block-chord harmony vocals and May's simple piano accompaniment make this an effective, quieter song in Queen's repertoire.

'Misfire' (John Deacon)

John Deacon's first song for Queen: concise, unassuming and effective. The composer plays the opening acoustic guitar (repeating G and C chords) with triple-tracked harmonic guitars from Brian May. The vocals start with the short chorus ('don't you misfire'). The verse is equally short, leading to a guitar solo played by Deacon himself. Deacon plays both guitar and bass on other self-penned songs such as 'You and I', 'Spread Your Wings', 'Who Needs You?', 'In Only Seven Days', 'Another One Bites the Dust', 'Need Your Loving Tonight', 'Back Chat', 'I Want to Break Free' and 'My Life Has Been Saved'.

The song then repeats itself in a higher key, adding a carefully arranged finale as the tune rises through uplifting step changes. 'Misfire' is a lovely loose song, and John Deacon would add many changes of pace and style in every Queen album to follow. His role as the 'secret weapon' is established here.

'Bring Back that Leroy Brown' (Freddie Mercury)

A hilarious lounge-jazz shuffle, springing from Jim Croce's 1972 hit 'Bad, Bad Leroy Brown'. It's the first of Mercury's vaudeville / Tin Pan Alley songs with added banjolele, barbershop vocal harmonies and a busy bass line doubled by the piano left hand. The lead vocal is remarkable – in this one song, Mercury sings a high A and low C three octaves below ('gonna bring that Leroy Brown').

Amazingly, this song was performed live between 1974 and 1977, in a truncated, mostly instrumental version, complete with a banjolele interlude worthy of *This Is Spinal Tap*.

An 'a capella' mix was released on the 1991 re-issue of *Sheer Heart Attack*. This isolates the vocals and highlights the intricacy of the backing vocals which sound almost 100% Freddie. An edited version was released as part of *The eYe* video game.

'She Makes Me (Stormtrooper in Stilettos)' (Brian May)

A slow, dense song, mostly alternating between the chords of D and A, but with an unexpected drop to Em7 in the verse ('she is my love'), and a more complex, proggy bridge section ('who knows where my dreams will end?'). Freddie does not take part.

The final seconds have a lovely dissonance which creates a tension that's never quite resolved.

'In the Lap of the Gods ... Revisited' (Freddie Mercury)

A dramatic, anthemic sing-along with a tightly arranged rhythm section: their first attempt at 'We Are the Champions'. We hear Freddie's lovely lyrical piano playing, Brian's big Red Special chords and a beautifully loud and melodic chorus reminiscent of Mott the Hoople's 'All the Young Dudes'. Queen toured with Mott the Hoople in March, April and May 1974: recording of *Sheer Heart Attack* started in July 1974.

Other than re-using the track's title, there seems to no musical or lyrical connection to 'In the Lap of the Gods'.

'In the Lap of the Gods ... Revisited' was performed live between 1974 and 1977, and again in 1986. It was also performed with Adam Lambert in 2014-2015. An edited and remixed version was released as part of *The eYe* video game. The edit starts mid-way through the track and the backing fades early giving an unaccompanied Freddie vocal for the last few seconds.

Footnotes

[1] Coon had been the subject of Robert Wyatt's beguiling 'O Caroline', recorded in 1972.

[2] Interview with Caroline Coon, *Melody Maker*.

[3] Mike West, *Queen – The First Five Years*, 1981.

[4] *Queen* didn't chart in the UK until 30 March 1974 – eight months after its release – following the success of 'Seven Seas of Rhye'. Its high of 24 was in January 1976, in the wake of 'Bohemian Rhapsody'.

[5] *Guitar Magazine*, August 1973.

[6] *Uncut*, March 2011.

[7] commentary on *Absolute Greatest*, 2009.

[8] *Music Star*, August 1974.

[9] *Guitar World*, 1998.

[10] Mike Oldfield's album was in the top 30 when *Queen II* was recorded.

[11] w/c 7 April 1974. The top ten that week was 1. 'Seasons in the Sun' by Terry Jacks; 2. 'Billy Don't Be a Hero' by Paper Lace; 3. 'Remember Me This Way' by

Gary Glitter (we'd rather not); 4. 'Everyday' by Slade; 5. 'Angel Face' by Glitter Band; 6. 'Emma' by Hot Chocolate; 7. 'You Are Everything' by Diana Ross and Marvin Gaye; 8. 'The Cat Crept In' by Mud; 9. 'The Most Beautiful Girl in the World' by Charlie Rich; 10. 'Seven Seas of Rhye' by Queen. Queen's song dropped to no. 14 the following week – displaced by The Wombles and Little Jimmy Osmond. 'Waterloo' by Abba was a new entry that week also. Ah, the 1970s.

[12] As quoted in *As It Began* by Jacky Gunn and Jim Jenkins (1992).

[13] *Classic Albums*, 2005.

[14] commentary on *Absolute Greatest*, 2009.

[15] Freddie Mercury, interview with Caroline Coon, *Melody Maker*, December 1974.

[16] Commentary on *Absolute Greatest*, 2009.

1975–1978: We Are the Champions

Queen's first three albums, attendant hit singles and 79-date world tour had pushed them into the public consciousness. *Sheer Heart Attack* not only gave Queen the commercial success they craved but also laid the foundation for the next phase: global domination. The trilogy of *A Night at the Opera*, *A Day at the Races* and *News of the World*, released in November 1975, December 1976 and October 1977 respectively, gave us thirty-one classic Queen songs, with hardly a mis-step from start to finish.

And yet the four band members were signed to Trident earning a weekly salary. Their lawyer, Jim Beach, extracted them from their contract and the band was able to make their magnum opus, *A Night at The Opera*, without distraction or financial pressure.

Queen would spend four months recording what many consider to be their best album.

A Night at the Opera (1975)

Personnel:
Freddie Mercury: lead vocals, backing vocals, piano
Brian May: electric guitar, acoustic guitar, lead vocals, backing vocals, koto, harp, ukulele
Roger Taylor: drums, lead vocals, backing vocals, percussion, electric guitar
John Deacon: bass guitar, electric piano, double bass.
Recorded in October 1974 at Trident Studios, London ('God Save the Queen'); August-September 1975 at Rockfield, Wales; September to November 1975 at Sarm, Roundhouse Studios, Trident Studios, Olympic Studios, Scorpio and Lansdowne, London. Produced by Roy Thomas Baker and Queen.
UK release date: 21 November 1975. US release date: 2 December 1975.
Highest chart places: UK: 1, USA: 4.

If you take it seriously then *A Night at the Opera* is utterly ridiculous – pretentious, silly overblown nonsense. If you don't, it's smart, creative, camp and a great deal of fun. Either way *A Night at the Opera* would change the lives of the four men in Queen.

'We needed a big turning point,' said Roger Taylor in 2005. 'And so, we banked everything on [that] album.'

'It took off like a rocket,' remarks Brian May. 'Suddenly we were in demand. Suddenly it looked like we wouldn't be in debt. Incredible.' [1]

The most expensive album ever recorded thus far was made at six studios, including Trident once again and the famous Rockfield in South Wales. With a deadline to meet, the album was finished three weeks before release date with the band working in three studios simultaneously, with final mixing at Sarm East in London.

A Night at the Opera was Queen's first no. 1 album, their first to achieve Platinum sales and their first top five album in the US.

A Night at the Opera was a record that seemed to come from everywhere and nowhere. From the beautiful, rippling arpeggios of 'Death on Two Legs', to the Noël Cowardesque frippery of 'Lazing on a Sunday Afternoon' and 'Seaside Rendezvous' (all three fabulous, in case you've never caught them); from 'Bohemian Rhapsody' with its unprecedented fusion of multi-layered operatic vocals and thunderous rock, to May's concluding rendition of the national anthem – it all felt wonderfully new, and has lost none of its sparkle.
Mark Monahan, *The Telegraph*, October 2015

'Death on Two Legs (Dedicated to...)' (Freddie Mercury)
Also released on *Queen's First EP* 20 May 1977. UK 17.
'Death on Two Legs (Dedicated to...)' is a spiteful but comical dismissal to the band's former manager Norman Sheffield. The powerful arrangement, with its opening piano arpeggios, tense, wide-open guitar riffing (written by Mercury on piano and transcribed to guitar), complex drum patterns, wheezing bowed double bass (under the intro's growling guitar riffs), overlapping vocal tracks and typically catchy melodies hides some vicious lyrics: 'You suck my blood like a leech' and 'You're a sewer rat decaying in a cesspool of pride'.

'I decided that if I wanted to stress something strongly I might as well go the whole hog and not compromise,' Freddie told *Sounds* in 1976. 'When the others first heard it, they were in a state of shock. But ... I was completely engrossed in it, swimming in it. Wow, I was a demon for a few days! Initially it going to have the intro, then everything [would] stop and the words YOU-SUCK-MY ... but that was going too far.'

'There's a sense of humour to it,' agreed Brian May. 'But there was a lot of anger there. I think we were taken back by how vicious Freddie wanted it to be.' [2]

The song was performed live from 1977 to 1981, then occasionally in 1982, usually as the opening part of a medley with 'Killer Queen'. The version on *Live Killers* is particularly tight. No-one sings 'you can kiss my ass goodbye' quite like Freddie Mercury!

Edited and instrumental versions of 'Death on Two Legs (Dedicated to...)' were released as part of *The eYe* video game.

'Lazing on a Sunday Afternoon' (Freddie Mercury)
The first of three up-tempo, jazzy vaudeville songs on *A Night at the Opera*, alongside 'Seaside Rendezvous' and 'My Melancholy Blues'. 'Lazing on a Sunday Afternoon' is short, funny, joyful and surprisingly complex, in marked contrast to the preceding 'Death on Two Legs (Dedicated to...)'. The backing vocals are lush, and the brief guitar solo is a harmonised variant of the vocal melody. If this song was a second longer it would be too much. As it is, embrace Queen's nonsense songs in the manner they were written – as fun interludes and nothing more. Don't take them seriously for a moment.

Part of the live set in 1975-1976.

'I'm In Love with My Car' (Roger Taylor)

Released as a single b-side on 31 October 1975 (UK and US), b/w 'Bohemian Rhapsody'.

This hard rock waltz became one of Queen's most famous album tracks after it was released as the b-side to 'Bohemian Rhapsody'. Roger Taylor wrote the song and sings lead (double-tracked throughout), all the backing vocals and, for the first time on a Queen record, plays electric guitar.

Whereas 'Lazing on a Sunday Afternoon' uses 19 different chords, 'I'm In Love with My Car' mostly gets away with four – Em, G, D and C – and uses the common I-III-VII-VI progression also heard in songs as varied as 'Call Me' (Blondie), 'Let Me Entertain You' (Robbie Williams), 'Polly' (Nirvana), 'Sunday Bloody Sunday' (U2), Call on Me' (Eric Prydz), 'Good Feeling' (Flo Rida), 'Just Dance' (Lady Gaga) and 'Fall to Pieces' (Avril Lavigne). And as with 'Tenement Funster', the verses and chorus use the same chord progressions. There is some trademark percussive piano from Freddie Mercury in the introduction and fade-out.

'I made a rough demo of it and took it round to Brian and said, 'what do you think of that?'', said Roger Taylor. 'He looked at me and said, 'you are joking, aren't you?'. It was slightly different from your average rock song. It's in 6/8-time, waltz time, which has a certain unstoppable rolling quality.' [3]

'What could have been a throwaway little ditty, jokingly dedicated to Queen's roadie,' writes Robert Ham, 'became one of the band's most searing and most beloved.' [4]

'I'm In Love with My Car' was performed in concert, with Taylor singing and drumming, from autumn 1977 to the end of 1981. It was a regular part of the tours with Paul Rodgers, as well as some of the dates with Adam Lambert.

A hybrid version, a combination of the single and album versions, is on *Queen Rocks*, released 3 November 1997 – this is the album version with the sound effects from the single version at the beginning. An excellent remix is on the 1991 re-release of *A Night at the Opera*. This starts with the harmonies from the chorus before the familiar intro kicks in – the whole song is louder and rockier with a fabulous up-front drum sound. A further remix on the 2011 re-release of *A Night at the Opera* – the 'guitar and vocal mix' – enables the listener to pick out Taylor's rhythm guitar and enjoy his outstanding lead vocals and harmonies.

'You're My Best Friend' (John Deacon)

Released as a single a-side, 18 May 1976 (UK and US), b/w "39'. UK: 7. US: 16. Released on *Greatest Hits*, 1981.

A perfect three-minute pop song driven by John Deacon's lop-sided Fender Rhodes electric piano playing. It was released as Queen's follow-up single to 'Bohemian Rhapsody' – a tender love letter from John Deacon to his wife Veronica.

"You're My Best Friend' is every inch a Queen song, 'suggests Phil Chapman in *The Dead Straight Guide to Queen* (2017). 'Freddie Mercury delivered John's lyrics with the same level of commitment as if he'd written them himself. Perhaps they resonated with his own love for Mary Austin.'

Mark Blake adds: "'You're My Best Friend' managed to sound unlike anything Queen had done before, but still wholly convincing: a trick the band would achieve again and again in years to come.'

'He was always the dark horse,' says Brian May. 'He would come in and we would say 'have you got anything, John?'. He'd say 'I've got this' ... 'Another One Bites the Dust', 'You're My Best Friend', 'I Want to Break Free' ... big, big hits.' [5]

'I remember seeing Donnie and Marie Osmond singing this on TV and thinking 'oh no, it's all gone terribly wrong'' laughs Roger Taylor. [6]

Queen's arrangement features 3-part and 4-part guitar lead and a very melodic bass line. The master tapes show that the electric piano part was double-tracked: there is significant bleed from the drums on one of these, but not the other. Freddie's superb lead vocal has embellishments and glissandos backed up by 3-part and 4-part harmonies. It's impossible not to sing along.

Even Queen's most fanatical worshippers might not list sincerity among Freddie Mercury and co's greatest qualities. So, step up bassist John Deacon, who wrote this wonderfully sincere tribute to his wife Veronica while trying to learn how to play the Wurlitzer electric piano. Mercury matches him all the way, too, as he bathes the song in complex, lilting Beach Boys-style harmonies and sings the lead with uncharacteristic restraint. It's a rare rock song that concludes 'I'm happy at home' and means it.
1000 Songs Everyone Must Hear, *The Guardian*, March 2009

'You're My Best Friend' was a set regular from 1976 to 1981. A remix is on the 1991 re-release of *A Night at the Opera*. It sounds almost identical to the 1976 version, with Freddie's vocal pushed forward, some echo on the snare drum and different placement of the lead guitar. A karaoke version, with lead vocals removed, but backing vocals retained has been released in Japan on the album *Greatest Karaoke Hits*. This same remix – labelled 'backing track mix' – is on the 2011 re-release of *A Night at the Opera*.

"39' (Brian May)
Released as a single b-side, 18 May 1976 (UK and US), b/w 'Your My Best Friend'.

"39' is a folky sci-fi parable, based rather obviously on Bob Dylan's 'When the Ship Comes In'. The song tells the story of a group of twenty explorers who embark on a year-long voyage into space. On their return one hundred years have passed, their loved ones have died, and they are about the same age as their grandchildren. May was inspired to write the song by the Herman Hesse novel *Siddhartha*.

'A man leaves his hometown and has lots of travels and then comes back and observes his hometown from the other side of the river,' explained Brian May when interviewed on BBC Radio One in 1983. 'He sees it in a different light having been away and experienced all those different things.'

'It's very, very unlike Queen really,' Freddie observed to *Record Mirror* in 1976. 'I think it's going to the b-side for 'You're My Best Friend'. It's something Brian wanted to do and that's nice.'

"39' was a set regular from 1976 to 1981: a change of pace in the middle of the show often paired with 'Love of My Life' and sometimes either 'My Melancholy Blues' or 'Dreamer's Ball'. All four band members would come to the front of the stage, with Deacon on bass, Mercury singing lead, Taylor singing backing vocals and playing tambourine and bass drum, and May, seated, playing 12-string guitar and singing backing vocals. "39' was sung, alone, by Brian May on the tours with Paul Rodgers and Adam Lambert.

'Sweet Lady' (Brian May)
The only really heavy song on the album – this rocker with waltz-time verses and straight-time middle 8 is infamous for the lyric 'You call me sweet like I'm some kind of cheese, waiting on the shelf'.

Performed regularly in concert from November 1975 to June 1977.

An edited version was released as part of *The eYe* video game.

'Seaside Rendezvous' (Freddie Mercury)
A fun up-tempo song, just piano, drums and vocals. The woodwind and brass arrangements are multi-tracked vocal performances by Freddie and Roger respectively. Freddie gives a masterclass in vocal technique – bent notes, vibrato, falsetto – and Taylor's drumming has a light touch.

'It was meant to be cod,' Taylor says, 'and cod it was.' [7]

'The Prophet's Song' (Brian May)
'One of my favourite songs of all time. Period' – Queen's producer Roy Thomas Baker, *Classic Albums*, 2005

Started during sessions for *Queen II* with the title 'People of the Earth', the monumental 'The Prophet's Song' is Queen's penultimate progressive rock epic following the likes of 'Doing All Right', 'My Fairy King', 'White Queen (As It Began)' and 'The March of the Black Queen'. Fans would need to wait sixteen years for their next and last.

"The Prophet's Song' is based around the drop-D tuning,' says Brian May, 'and I became fascinated by what you could do with that. It gives the guitar a lot more depth; a real doomy kind of growl. The end of each riff was different. That was a very Queen thing – we liked to never repeat ourselves, even within the context of a song ... you would always hear something different every time the chorus came around. That became a little trademark, I suppose.' [8]

'The Prophet's Song' differs from other long-form songs of the first half of the

1970s in that rather than a lengthy extemporised solo section we move through many different sections.

0:00 Wind effects – the studio's air conditioning unit with a phaser effect – take us into a mix of 12-string guitar playing the theme from the chorus and an overdubbed toy koto, a traditional Japanese stringed musical instrument.

0:38 The first chorus – Freddie's subtle vocal is accompanied by acoustic guitar, itself shadowed by electric rhythm. The rhythm section and vocal harmonies enter on the last phrase: 'listen to the wise *man*'.

0:51 The first verse is four-square with mystical lyrics from a dream that Brian May had – 'I dreamed I saw on a moonlit stair / spreading his hands on the multitude there'. A primitive arrangement starts to blossom in the second stanza as more guitars enter along with Taylor's dynamic drumming. Mercury's vocal line lifts and pushes towards...

1:29 The second chorus – a variant on the first.

1:42 The third chorus, now with vocals in block harmonies and different lyrics – building through the first two minutes, the song is now at full power.

1:56 A return to the verse with wonderfully arranged harmonic guitars in the second half.

2:29 The fourth chorus – now with wider harmonies. This chorus ends on different key ('listen to the good *land*') to join to the bridge.

2:41 The first bridge ('and two by two') is a variant of the chorus, just different enough to keep the listener off balance.

2:57 The second bridge ('flee for your life') has a powerful Zeppelin-meets-the-Beatles descending guitar / bass.

3:25 The vocal canon – Freddie Mercury's amazing solo-through-delay vocal eventually transforms into a call-response choir. This was carefully worked out by Brian May beforehand; parts are taken from the 'around around' section from 'Now I'm Here'. Two and a half minutes of bliss which could only be Queen.

5:52 May's wah-wah guitar solo driven by power chords, crashing drums and harmonized guitar.

6:50 A reprise of the last phrase of the verse – 'God gave you grace to purge this place / and peace all around may be your fortune'.

6:57 The fifth chorus, with many overdubbed guitars and vocals.

7:10 The sixth chorus, with May's solo reprise in the first half and final blossoming vocal harmony.

7:24 The conclusion – spinning electric guitar loops and a blast of drums, then a reprise of the chorus theme on acoustic guitar and koto finishing with part of the introduction for 'Love of My Life'.

'The Prophet's Song' was performed live many times in 1975, 1976, 1977 and 1978.

'Love of My Life' (Freddie Mercury)

Live version, recorded at Festhalle Frankfurt, 2 February 1979, released as a single a-side, 29 June 1979. UK 63.

Queen's best love song by a country mile. This exquisite ballad was famously written for Mary Austin, with whom Freddie had a long-term relationship in the early 1970s. [8]

Freddie Mercury's complex and beautiful classically-inspired piano part has echoes of Chopin and Beethoven and his multiple harmony backing vocals are simply beautiful. Brian May contributes subtle electric guitar phrases in the tone and style of cello.

'Making records is often tedious and repetitive,' says long-time roadie Peter Hince. 'During the recording of *A Night at the Opera* I spent my days and nights commuting across London to various studios. I was picking up an antique harp for Brian to play on 'Love of My Life', from an equally ancient woman in Barnes, when I thought 'Queen is a rock band – is this rock 'n' roll?" [9]

Matt Richards and Mark Langthorne say, in *Somebody to Love* (2017), that ex-Queen manager John Reid told them that 'Love of My Life' is about David Minns, Freddie's boyfriend from 1975-1976. Whilst we can be fairly certain 'Good Old-Fashioned Lover Boy' was written for Minns, it seems much more likely that Mary Austin is the subject of 'Love of My Life'.

Freddie himself said (in an undated press cutting but from around the time of the release of *A Night at the Opera*): 'I suppose I do write a lot of sad songs, but that doesn't mean I feel that way myself. I really enjoy writing those songs but, again, there isn't necessarily any connection between the music and my life. 'Love of My Life', for instance, I simply made up. There's nothing personal about it. Am I making sense? What I mean is, writing those sad songs makes me happy. To me, they're fun, so it all fits in. I just happen to like that kind of music.'

Of course, what he said then and what he actually felt when writing the song do not need to tally: Freddie never gave too much away in interviews.

First performed in concert in October 1977, and a permanent addition until the last concerts in 1986, 'Love of My Life' was rearranged for 12-string guitar and was always sung with real feeling by Freddie. As seen at Wembley and Knebworth in 1986, it takes a special performer and a special song to hold upwards of 72,000 in thrall with just voice and guitar.

Freddie would speak the lines 'I still love you' in live performances – and use the same words and inflection at the end of 'These Are the Days of Our Lives' as his life was drawing to a close.

From 2005 it was a set regular, sung by May. In 2017, May was joined by audio and video of Freddie Mercury for the last verse (taken from the second 1986 Wembley show). What should be cringingly embarrassing is very moving indeed and a powerful tribute to lost love everywhere.

An edited version, just the harp flourish, was released as part of *The eYe* video game.

If anyone is not convinced by the power, invention, craft and dynamism of mid-period Queen, then sit them down and simply play 'The Prophet's Song' and 'Love of My Life'.

'Good Company' (Brian May)

Written as a kind of ukulele-banjo shuffle, 'Good Company' has no input at all from Freddie Mercury: Brian May sings and plays everything except bass and drums.

The conclusion has a heavily arranged jazz band sound, with each instrument – trumpets, clarinets, trombones – played by May on his Red Special, sometimes one note at a time.

'When it came to doing the solo part for 'Good Company'', he says 'I wanted it to sound like a jazz band, and I wanted the guitar to be the jazz band. Every note was done separately to get the proper sounds of clarinet, trumpet, trombone and bells. It was very painstaking, but a lot of fun because it had never been done before.' [10]

'Bohemian Rhapsody' (Freddie Mercury)

Released as a single a-side, 31 October 1975 (UK and US), b/w 'I'm In Love with My Car'. UK: 1. US: 9. Released on *Greatest Hits*, 1981. Released as a single a-side, 2 December 1991 (UK and US), b/w 'These Are the Days of Our Lives'. UK: 1. US: 2.

'Bohemian Rhapsody' is surely the song that defines Queen more than any other. Those who listened to their first three albums could trace the lineage of 'Bohemian Rhapsody' through songs such as 'My Fairy King', 'The Fairy Feller's Master-Stroke', 'The Night Comes Down', 'Nevermore' and 'The March of the Black Queen'. None of these was released as single. Anyone listening to 'Bohemian Rhapsody' on the radio for the first time in late 1975 must have been stopped in their tracks by its startling originality.

For some, 'Bohemian Rhapsody' represents the work of a rebel genius who, by refusing the constraints his chosen genre, created an otherworldly opus full of devils, heretics and shivering spines. For others, the track is a pretentious overly long example of a rampant ego foisting his worst excesses upon the world. In short, 'Bohemian Rhapsody' can divide a room more quickly than religion or politics.
Martin Power, *The Complete Guide to the Music of Queen*, 2006

According to Chris Smith, briefly the keyboard player in Smile, Mercury started developing 'Bohemian Rhapsody' in 1968-1969. The opening ballad section was known as 'The Cowboy Song' and contained the 'mama' lyrics that were included in the completed version.

Recording started at Rockfield on 24 August 1975. The backing track was completed in two halves, each a single take – piano, bass and drums. A

30-second strip of blank tape for a to-be-determined central segment – what was already being called 'the opera section' – split the two halves.

0:00   The four-part *a capella* introduction immediately puts us on our guard – not only this music such as we've never heard before, but the lyrics ask us uncomfortable questions ('Is this the real life? Is this just fantasy?'). The first phrase is also in 9/8 time; a very rare example of an unusual time signature in a Queen song.

0:48   The ballad section, with wide open intervals in B flat, possibly worked out initially on guitar. Only bass is used as accompaniment until the second half of the first verse when drums and double-tracked rhythm guitars enter adding dynamic variation.

1:49   The second verse of the ballad section, with counter melodies from the lead guitar and a second Freddie vocal. The sound effect at 2.02 after 'shivers down my spine' is a strum across May's Red Special guitar strings above the nut.

2:35   First guitar solo, accompanied by fat low notes on a second guitar. The solo climbs higher, with fast hammer-ons and pull-offs, neatly resolving to the dominant key of the next section.

3:02   The 'opera' section, starting with four-square piano chords taken from the middle part of The Beatles' 'A Day in the Life'. Scaramouche, fandango, Bismillah, mamma mia, Beelzebub … absolute nonsense which somehow hangs together. The central 'Galileo' section was planned as a double-tracked Freddie Mercury self-duet but was sensibly replaced later by the familiar Taylor / Mercury version. The 'no no no' harmonies are simply absurd, and the falsetto on the final 'for me' is the highest note in any Queen song. The master tapes include unused guitar fills at the beginning of this section.

4:07   The 'rock' section, full of power chords, fast riffs, grinding bass and a grunting Freddie lead vocal, which breaks on 'to die' – there are four lead vocal tracks on the master at this stage, but the band and producer Roy Thomas Baker choose this to use dropped-in overdub.

4:54   The ascending piano resolves to a lead guitar part, underpinned by 'ooh yeah' harmonies, a wistful reprise of the 'nothing really matters' line, some sweet guitar phrases and the concluding 'any way the wind blows' (and gong).

And so, the music world is transformed in five minutes and 54 seconds.

It seems that 'Bohemian Rhapsody' was always planned as a single: an edit was considered at EMI's request.

'We listened to it over and over again,' John Deacon commented in 1977, 'And there was no way we could edit it. We tried a few ideas but if you edited it you always lost some part of the song, so we had to leave it all in.'

Sense prevailed, and the full-length track dominated the UK charts for weeks in late 1975. The song entered the chart at 47 the week after it was released, then jumped to 17 on 9 November, and 9 on 16 November. The now famous accompanying film was shown on *Top of the Pops* on 20 November 1975 and the next week 'Bohemian Rhapsody' began a nine-week run at number one, at that time the second longest continuous run at the top of the pile in UK chart history.

To underline the song's universal appeal, when the long-running BBC radio programme *Desert Island Discs* tallied music choices from its castaways between 1942 and 2012, 'Bohemian Rhapsody' proved to be one of only two non-classical pieces in the top ten. [11]

'Bohemian Rhapsody' has been performed at every Queen concert from late 1975 onwards. Its complex arrangement, and multi-tracked vocal sections, necessitated some re-arrangements. On the tour to promote *A Night at the Opera* (November 1975 to April 1976), the song was split into three sections. A recording of the operatic middle section was used to open the show, with the hard rock section comprising the first live piece. The ballad sections would form part of a medley with 'Killer Queen' and 'The March of the Black Queen' later in the show. From 1977, the song would be performed from the opening ballad through to the start of the operatic section, a recording of the middle section would be accompanied by a light show, then the band would return to conclude the song. The introductory 'is this the real life' section was never performed, although Freddie Mercury would sometimes sing the opening lines to 'Mustapha', or the piano introduction to 'Death on Two Legs' instead. It was a set regular on the tours with Paul Rodgers and Adam Lambert. Different arrangements, both using archive recordings of Freddie Mercury, would be utilised.

A version with The Muppets (new vocal over original backing track with some verses edited out), credited to Queen + The Muppets, was released as a download in 2009. UK: 32. The Muppets vocals are performed by Bill Barretta, Dave Goelz, Eric Jacobson, David Rudman, Matt Vogel and Steve Whitmire. An 'a capella mix' of the operatic section is on the 2011 re-release of *A Night at the Opera*.

Seek out William Shatner's unique cover version. Forget about Kanye West.

'God Save the Queen' (Trad. arr May)
This version of the British National Anthem was recorded a few days before Queen's 1974 UK tour, expressly to conclude their concerts, played over the PA as the band took their bows.

Other contemporary songs
'The Man from Manhattan'
This is not a Queen song, but it's worthy of mention here as a rare occasion when one of the band produced a session for someone else. Eddie Howell was a singer-songwriter signed to Warner Bros. who had released a handful of singles and an album in 1975. As the story goes, he asked Freddie Mercury

to produce his single 'The Man from Manhattan' and not only did Mercury agree, but Brian May decided to take part as well. The song was recorded in August 1975 at Sarm East Studios. The bridge is very Queen indeed with multi-layered harmony vocals. There are two excellent short guitar solos and some Queenesque changes in dynamics and tempo. The song is available on the exhaustive Freddie box set *The Solo Collection* released in 2000.

Eddie Howell – acoustic guitar, vocals / Freddie Mercury - piano, backing vocals / Brian May - guitar / Barry De Sousa - drums / Jerome Rimson – bass

A Day at the Races (1976)
Personnel:
Freddie Mercury: lead vocals, backing vocals, piano
Brian May: electric guitar, acoustic guitar, lead vocals, backing vocals, keyboards
Roger Taylor: drums, lead vocals, backing vocals, percussion, electric guitar
John Deacon: bass, acoustic guitar
+ Mike Stone – additional vocals on 'Good Old-Fashioned Lover Boy'.
Recorded July to November 1976 at The Manor, Oxfordshire, and Sarm Studios, Wessex Studios and Advision Studios, London. Produced by Roy Thomas Baker and Queen.
UK release date: 10 December 1976. US release date: 18 December 1976.
Highest chart places: UK: 1, USA: 5.

A Day at the Races is Queen's first self-produced album, and the second to borrow its title from a film by the Marx Brothers. It's a companion to, or a continuation of, *A Night at the Opera* rather than a direct sequel, recorded at many of the same studios. *A Day at the Races* would explore many of the same musical styles and genres but there are fewer new ideas than any previous Queen album: 'You and I' is similar to 'You're My Best Friend', 'You Take My Breath Away' is an update of 'Love of My Life', 'Millionaire Waltz' apes 'Bohemian Rhapsody', 'Long Away' looks back to '"39', 'Good Old-Fashioned Lover Boy' is a rewrite of 'Lazing on a Sunday Afternoon' … but they do deliver a classic hit single in 'Somebody to Love'.

The band's writing has settled into more accessible love lyrics rather than dealing with sci-fi, fairy stories or rats. '[It] comprised brisk, expensive-sounding pop-rock,' writes Mark Blake, 'with singles that would sit comfortably on a radio playlist between Electric Light Orchestra, Rod Stewart or Wings.'

One notable new recording venue was Richard Branson's Manor Studios in Shipton-on-Cherwell, Oxfordshire – Queen recorded backing vocals there in autumn 1976.

'Tie Your Mother Down' (Brian May)
Released as a single a-side, 4 March 1977, b/w 'You and I'. UK: 31. US: 49.
Originally written on acoustic guitar in autumn 1971 whilst Brian May was in Tenerife working on his PhD, by 1976 'Tie Your Mother Down' is a rip-roaring,

mean, bluesy hard rocker, brought out whenever the band needed to display their heavier side. May's metallic slide guitar breaks in the second half of his guitar solo are astounding.

> *'Tie Your Mother Down' is pretty feisty, giving Mercury a sharp break from kitsch which in fact allows him to prove himself not a bad rock vocalist.*
> Nick Kent, *NME*, December 1976

Usually either opening the set, or one of the opening brace, 'Tie Your Mother Down' was a set regular from summer 1976, right through to the last gigs with Freddie in 1986. The opening fanfare was played from the unfinished album at the band's important Hyde Park show in 1976 with the as-yet-unrecorded 'Tie Your Mother Down' near to the end of the set of the other shows that summer. It was also a perennial on the tours with Paul Rodgers (something of a bellow) and Adam Lambert (directly channelling Freddie).

The long introduction, before Brian May's famous guitar riff, is a variant of 'White Man' followed by a version of the ascending harmonies from the end of Pink Floyd's 'Echoes' (or perhaps from 'Round and Round' by Aerosmith).

The single version removes the long intro, kicking off with the riff. Trent Reznor remixed 'Tie Your Mother Down' in 1991, for a withdrawn promo CD. It removes Brian May's guitar riff almost completely and sounds like Freddie singing with Nine Inch Nails. It's very good indeed. Imagine that! A new remix is on the 1991 re-release of *A Day at the Races*. This adds lots of echo on the vocals. An edited version, just the fanfare introduction, was released as part of *The eYe* video game. There is also the 'Air guitar version', which includes a sample of 'We Will Rock You', released on *The Best Air Guitar Album in the World … Ever!*, *Vol. 1* in 2001, and a further remix, the 'backing track mix', is on the 2011 re-release of *A Day at the Races*.

'You Take My Breath Away' (Freddie Mercury)
'You Take My Breath Away' is one of Mercury's best ballads, sung without irony or pomp. Immaculate and atmospheric multi-layered backing vocals, all by Mercury, accompany a simple piano backing, with flashes of guitar and percussion. The vocal interlude between 'You Take My Breath Away' and 'Long Away' repeats the words 'take my breath' in reverse, crossfading to a repeated 'you take my (breath away)'. This song is a logical extension of 'Lily of the Valley' from *Sheer Heart Attack*, and of the opening ballad section of 'Bohemian Rhapsody'. But, 'You Take My Breath Away' is a small gem of a song, amongst the very finest of Freddie's quieter moments.

'You Take My Breath Away' was debuted at the band's Hyde Park concert some weeks prior to the release of *A Day at the Races*. Freddie, balls out as usual, plays a brand new, unheard ballad in front of 150,000 fans – and they *listen*. It was then performed regularly in 1976 and 1977, starting with the piano intro and ending after the first chorus. A quite beautiful instrumental version – Freddie's piano track only – was included on the soundtrack to video game *The eYe* in 1998.

'Long Away' (Brian May)

Released as a single a-side, 7 June 1977 (US) b/w 'You and I'.

'Long Away' is cheerful filler, something of a sequel to "39" with a touch of Buddy Holly in arrangement and of early Beatles in vocal and accompanying electric 12-string guitar. 'Long Away' was never performed by the classic Queen line-up but Brian May added the song to his solo section of the Q+PR set twice in 2005 and twice in 2006.

"Long Away' is fairly decent folk-rock,' Nick Kent wrote in 1976. 'A jingle jangling guitar nod of the plectrum to The Byrds and a pleasant 'pop' melody, even if May's classic strangled Ostrich guitar tone (which he uses for all solos performed in the upper register of the fretboard) doesn't add anything.'

'The Millionaire Waltz' (Freddie Mercury)

The baroque, tongue-in-cheek 'The Millionaire Waltz' borrows generously from 'Bohemian Rhapsody'. The classical piano playing, huge vocal overdubs, and rock breakdown are all present and correct, this time in waltz time.

0:00 An instrumental introduction for piano (mostly in the right channel) and closely-miked melodic bass guitar (mostly in the left).

0:21 The verse starts with the well-used I-VI-II-V chord progression – see also 'Bohemian Rhapsody', 'Love of My Life', 'Hungry Heart', 'Blue Moon', 'What's Going On?', 'Without You' and countless others. Queen's trademark tightly arranged harmony vocals and guitars close this section.

0:53 A 'ballad' section, again just piano, vocals and bass. A clean, fluid lead guitar enters as the tempo increases and the arrangement thickens.

2:22 An abrupt change to a loud rock section (in 4/4), with Mercury and May at full throttle.

2:46 A switch back to waltz time, back to the piano chords of the introduction and to a guitar solo with a very old-time feel: listen to 'Oom pah pah' from *Oliver!* by Lionel Bart. May's hammers-on are very fluid. The closing section has multiple harmonised guitar parts.

3:26 A melancholic bridge section ('my fine friend') richly orchestrated with many multitracked guitars. May's heavily arranged lead guitar breaks include tricky triplet arpeggios in ¾ time, with many overdubs – May sounds like a one-man jazz band in places (shades of 'Good Company').

4:38 Closing section with hammering drums and power chords and a very definite slam-the-door ending.

'The Millionaire Waltz' was a set regular in 1977 and 1978. The live version was shortened: the first verse leads directly to the rock section and the last verse is omitted.

'You and I' (John Deacon)

Released as a single b-side, 4 March 1977 (UK), b/w 'Tie Your Mother Down'.
Released as a single b-side, 7 June 1977 (US) b/w 'Long Away'.

Deacon's lone contribution to *A Day at the Races* starts with a jaunty piano part and stereo drum patterns before settling down into a melodic, upbeat mid-paced rocker. It builds to a densely orchestrated second half with Queen's patent multi-tracked vocals and guitars. It might be Queen-by-numbers in places, but 'You and I' is unduly one of the forgotten songs of the Queen catalogue.

'Somebody to Love' (Freddie Mercury)

Released as a single a-side, 12 November 1976, b/w 'White Man'. UK: 2. US: 13.
Released on *Greatest Hits,* 1981.
Broadway musical-meets-doowop-meets-Harlem-church-choir. The message of one of Queen's greatest singles is direct and universal – I work hard, why can't I find love? It is the complex layered vocal tracks that give this classic Queen song more than a hint of gospel. The arrangement of the backing vocals in the verses is particularly complex, yet effortlessly commercial.

'Ooh, each morning I get up I die a little
Can barely stand on my feet
(Take a look at yourself)
Take a look in the mirror and cry
(and cry)
Lord what you're doing to me (yeah yeah)'

It's remarkable that it's the combination of just three voices overdubbed many times that provides the 100-voice choir that drives the central section of 'Somebody to Love'.

Each phrase of this central gospel section thickens the sound: firstly, the main tune for bass voices; then with octave harmony and drums; harmonies in fifth and thirds; higher octaves added; higher thirds with handclaps; same again with oscillating last syllable; and again, with high notes on '...love'.

There's also Freddie's amazing high note in 'somebody *to...*', followed by the utter control of his delivery through the simultaneously electrifying and uplifting eleven notes of '...lo-oh-wo-wo-wo-wo-wove.'

'Somebody to Love' was introduced to the band's live set in January 1977 and performed regularly through to May 1984. It was also performed with Adam Lambert.

I particularly like 'Somebody to Love' – it was fantastic live when the band put more energy and rock into it. Fred said it was a far better piece of song writing than 'Bohemian Rhapsody'.
Peter 'Ratty' Hince, communication with the author, 2018

A remix is included on the 1991 re-release of *A Night at the Opera* – the backing vocals are pushed forward, the bass sounds fuller and masses of reverb have been added.

A nod must be given to George Michael who made a decent fist of the track at the 1992 tribute concert and scored a UK number one the following year. 'Aretha Franklin was Freddie's idol', says Brian May, 'And he wrote ['Somebody to Love'] with her in mind. I wonder if she's ever sung it?' [12]

'White Man' (Brian May)

Released as a single b-side, 12 November 1976, b/w 'Somebody to Love'. An ugly, unconvincing, ill-advised, over-sincere, social-historical critique.

"White Man' is an absurdly ham-brained attack on ... well you guessed it, out fair-skinned predecessors' predilection for carnage and rip-offs against Ethnic Folks of other inscrutable tints,' writes Nick Kent. "Ere but, wait a sec, Bri, that riff – I've heard that before somewheres. Led Zeppelin's 'When the Levee Breaks', to be exact, which Jimmy Page took from (and co-credited to) one Memphis Minnie, a wonderful black person. Roll dem' bones, boys – white man sings with forked tongue.' [13]

Performed live in 1977 and 1978.

'Good Old-Fashioned Lover Boy' (Freddie Mercury)

Released on *Queen's First EP*, 20 May 1977. UK 17. Released on *Greatest Hits*, 1981.

A wonderfully playful song, very much in the vein of 'You and I', but with a commercial chorus and staggeringly good vocal harmonies. The guitar solo has a sophisticated arrangement with harmonised melodies across the stereo image.

'Good Old-Fashioned Lover Boy' would be the lead track on *Queen's First EP*, released in May 1977. BBC radio seemed quite happy to broadcast the line: 'I learned my passion from the good old-fashioned school of lover boys'. Good for them.

Performed live in 1977 and 1978, 'Good Old-Fashioned Lover Boy' was re-recorded for the band's appearance on BBC's Top of the Pops on 16 June 1977. This version is faster and heavier, with some different lyrics, and Roger sings some vocals on the 'hey boy, where'd ya go' section. This is available on the 2011 re-issue of *A Night at the Opera*.

'Drowse' (Roger Taylor)

Roger Taylor's 'Drowse' is a lethargic lump of psychedelia that sounds unlike anything else in Queen's catalogue. It's a reminder of the diversity in the band's democratic song writing ethos, even if it's not a particularly engaging listen.

'Teo Torriatte (Let Us Cling Together)' (Brian May)

'Teo Torriatte (Let Us Cling Together)', was written and performed by Brian May on piano. It has a warm and sincere vocal from Freddie. Certainly, hearing him sing 'When I'm gone ...' has a genuine poignancy, but this is a weak album closer in comparison to, say, 'Seven Seas of Rhye', 'Bohemian Rhapsody', 'My Melancholy Blues' or 'Save Me'.

The song was a minor hit in Japan and was added to Japanese set-lists between 1978 and 1982, and again on tours with Paul Rodgers and Adam Lambert.

A new mix was prepared in 2004 for the Japanese *Jewels II* compilation. This is available on the 2011 re-issue of *A Night at the Opera*.

News of the World (1977)

Personnel:
Freddie Mercury: lead vocals, backing vocals, piano, cowbell
Brian May: electric guitar, acoustic guitar, lead vocals, backing vocals, maracas
Roger Taylor: drums, lead vocals, backing vocals, electric guitar, bass guitar
John Deacon: bass guitar, acoustic guitar.
Recorded between July and September 1977 at Basing Street Studios and Wessex Studios, London. Produced by Queen and Mike Stone.
UK release date: 28 October 1977. US release date: 1 November 1977.
Highest chart places: UK: 4, USA: 3.

Both 'Bohemian Rhapsody' and *A Night at the Opera* had opened the international market to Queen, and *A Day at the Races* went into the US top 5. But US reviews of *A Day at the Races* and the accompanying tour were not kind. The band's sixth album, *News of the World* was pitched against the angst of punk: 1977 was the year of *Never Mind the Bollocks*, but also of *Saturday Night Fever*. Queen's response, if perhaps unconsciously, was to strip down their sound, hold back on the overdubs and keep the songs as simple as possible.

Of course, with Queen, back-to-basics includes a cod-jazz ballad, a six-and-a-half-minute song divided into three acts, and a rumination on the death of Brian May's pet cat. But 'We Will Rock You' is as basic a song as you can imagine, and, throughout, the band's knack for melody and pomp is intact. Recorded in only ten weeks at two studios, song-writing was more or less divided equally between the four members. Co-incidentally or by design, two songs have no contribution at all from Freddie Mercury, another is co-sung, and a fourth has him on backing vocals only.

News of the World remains the band's biggest selling non-compilation album. The striking album artwork features an adaptation of the cover of the October 1953 edition of an American magazine called *Astounding Science Fiction* by respected science-fiction artist Frank Kelly Freas. The arresting depiction of a dispassionate giant robot plucking the band members from a shattered auditorium is among the most disquieting of any album artwork.

'We Will Rock You' (Brian May)
Released as a single a-side, 7 October 1977, b/w 'We Are the Champions'. UK: 2. US: 4. Released on *Greatest Hits*, 1981. Released as a single b-side, 25 February 1996, b/w 'Too Much Love Will Kill You'

'We Will Rock You' is a dumb song from this intelligent band – we might have forgiven 'We Will Rock You' if it was by, say, Kiss or Aerosmith. A song written in the future tense – other examples are very rare – 'We Will Rock You' is, I suppose, a rallying call describing life in three stages, moving from 'boy' to 'young man' to 'old man'. It's cheap, it's stupid, it's obnoxious, it's commercial. 'We Will Rock You' marks the first hint of Queen's move towards the blatant and bare-faced chart-grabbing songs of *The Game* and beyond.

'We Will Rock You' was recorded at Wessex. The 'boom boom cha' at the start [were] recorded by all available feet stomping on some wooden platforms while hands clapped the off beat in the cavernous room. The result was soaked in echo, multi-tracked and given some studio magic by engineer Mike Stone to create an introduction that has become an anthem.
Peter 'Ratty' Hince, *Queen Unseen*, 2015

Permanently added to the set in October 1977, usually as part of the final encore, 'We Will Rock You' was also performed with Paul Rodgers and Adam Lambert.

A fast version often opened shows between 1977 and 1982, with the familiar arrangement also being played later in the show. A live version recorded at Festhalle Frankfurt, 2 February 1979, was released as a single a-side in the US on 24 August 1979, b/w 'Let Me Entertain You' (*Live Killers* version) and as a single b-side in the UK on 5 October 1979, b/w 'Crazy Little Thing Called Love'. This fast version was also performed with Adam Lambert.

There are many other versions of 'We Will Rock You'. An alternative 'raw' version was released on the 2017 re-issue of *News of the World*. This has some studio chatter and the call for take one. It sounds like a different vocal take. The guitar solo is obviously a first attempt. The backing track of the released master was released on the 2017 re-issue of *News of the World*. This has a very full stereo sound but is empty without Freddie. 'We Will Rock You was remixed by Dakeyne, released on *DMC Classic Remixes*, January 1991. This is a DJ remix, using Queen's vocal track. The song was remixed by Rick Rubin for the 1991 re-issue of *News of the World*. Rubin's mix takes Mercury's vocal, replaces the stamping and clapping, adds elements from 'Tie Your Mother Down' and 'Stone Cold Crazy' and adds extra drums to create a kind of '90s version of the fast arrangement. It's fun. Several other mixes can be found on the 1991 US-only CD single, including 'Ruined Instrumental', 'Big Beat a Capella', 'Zulu

Scratch a Capella', 'Effects a Capella', 'Clap a Capella' and '12" mix'.
'We Will Rock You' has been re-recorded several times. The song was recorded for the BBC, 28 October 1977 as a medley with the fast version that was first played in concert in this period. It includes a reading from *Siddhartha* by Herman Hesse, supposedly a fortuitous accident. Released on *On Air*, 4 November 2016, this BBC version is possibly superior to the album cut. 'We Will Rock You' was re-recorded in 1999 with boyband Five; from the album *Invincible* (19 November 1999) and a UK no. 1 single (17 July 2000), credited to Five + Queen. Unspeakable. The song was re-recorded in 2003 with Australian vocalist John Farnham, released on *True Colours – The Official Album of The Rugby World Cup 2003* and Farnham's *One Voice – The Greatest Hits* album (also 2003). It is credited to Queen + John Farnham. Farnham has a powerful voice, and the extended arrangement is inventive. The song was partially re-recorded for a Pepsi advert in 2003 featuring additional vocals by Britney Spears, Beyonce Knowles and P!nk. Released as a promo CD in January 2004. We tried to pretend that this doesn't exist. A worthwhile version from 2012 mixes Freddie's vocals, the stamping and handclaps from the original version, newly recorded guitar from Brian, and piano and orchestrations from Helmut Von Lichten formerly of the group EL Posthumus. Credited to Queen + Von Lichten, this has been used for sports coverage in the US.

'There was probably a time when 'We Will Rock You' didn't exist,' writes Martin Power, 'but it's hard to remember exactly when.' [14]

'We Are the Champions' (Freddie Mercury)
Released as a single a-side, 7 October 1977, b/w 'We Will Rock You'. UK: 2. US: 4. Released on *Greatest Hits,* 1981. Released as a single b-side, 25 February 1996, b/w 'Too Much Love Will Kill You'.

Nothing less than a rock anthem, but with many nuances that other stadium-friendly songs don't have: a sophisticated arrangement with dramatic changes in dynamics; dissonance; many key changes; big choir-like harmonies; a wonderfully melodic bass line; the outstanding guitar arrangement in the second verse; and Freddie Mercury's expressive voice.

'When Fred strode into Shepperton Film Studios for rehearsals in summer 1977 and announced he had this football fan song,' writes Peter Hince, 'it was received with caution and an element of disbelief – what was he doing now? He had already seen the potential of his sporting anthemic idea and knew it could carry successfully into live shows.' [15]

'"We Are the Champions' is the Queen song that has always worked the band's fiercest detractors into a lather,' says Mark Blake, 'The song's shameless sentiment – bigger, better, more and damn the losers – was at odds with the prevailing musical mood of the time.'

'It's lovely to hear that 'We Are the Champions' is a song that's been taken up by football fans,' Freddie said to David Wigg, 1985, ''cause that's a winners' song. I can't believe that somebody else hasn't written a new song to take it over, you know?'

'We Are the Champions' is the catchiest song of all time, according to a study in 2011, carried out by Dr Alisun Pawley for her PhD at the University of York and Dr Daniel Müllensiefen of Goldsmiths University of London. Dr Pawley said:

Nightlife in northern England was a unique and fertile ground to observe sing-along behaviour. There are not many situations in society today that can you find people jumping up and down, belting out a tune at the top of their lungs. Although this is a cultural study, its empirical approach and scientific methods allowed us to uncover patterns in human behaviour. Freddy Mercury's vocal style typifies what we found inspires people to sing along – a full energy male voice, using a high chest voice and clearly pronounced words.

The song was permanently added to Queen's live set in October 1977, usually as the final encore. It was also performed with Paul Rodgers and Adam Lambert. 'We ended our live set with this song and it always felt like a fitting climax to an evening,' says Roger Taylor. [16]

A looser 'raw' version ('this will be take 37,000') was released on the 2017 re-issue of *News of the World*. This has much more guitar. The backing track of the finished mix is also available on the 2017 re-issue of *News of the World*. A 1991 CD promo single includes overdubbed snippets of a George Bush speech – released as 'We Are the Champions (Gulf War version)'. This Hollywood Records release was not approved by the band. 'We Are the Champions' has been remixed by Rick Rubin as 'We Are the Champions (Remix Ruined by Rick Rubin)' and released with 'We Will Rock You (Ruined by Rick Rubin')' in the US in 1991. It sounds like 'We Are the Champions' with the drum break from 'Funky Drummer' playing in the next room. The song was re-recorded by Taylor and May in early 2001 for the film *A Knight's Tale*. Vocals by Robbie Williams. Released 15 May 2001, credited to Robbie Williams + Queen. This is the same arrangement as the familiar hit but with the ex-Take That singer pummelling the song to death in a horrible American accent. Not even a full-bodied Brian May guitar solo lifts this above an embarrassing mess. Thankfully, plans for a Queen + Robbie Williams concert tour fell through.

'Sheer Heart Attack' (Roger Taylor)
Released as a single b-side, 10 February 1978 (UK), b/w 'Spread Your Wings'. Released as a single b-side, 25 April 1978 (US), b/w 'It's Late'. 74.

Started during sessions for the album *Sheer Heart Attack*, the energetic song 'Sheer Heart Attack' is a deliberately simple song. Roger Taylor plays everything except some liquid lead guitar lines from Brian May.

Roger had done a demo, and our usual practice was to use the demos as

a bed for the final track. Roger had sung it all, but the decision was made to get Freddie for the record. Roger was keen that Freddie sing it pretty much like the demo to retain the atmosphere. Freddie didn't find it that easy since it wasn't his natural style. But it's Freddie you hear doing the verses – double tracked. The choruses are, I think, all of us, but with Roger up front – the demo versions dominating – in fact it sounds to me like ALL Roger in the choruses in the mix now I listen to it...
Brian May on his website in 2003

'Sheer Heart Attack' was a regular in the live set from October 1977 through to the end of 1982, then revived occasionally in 1984 (five times). With 252 known live performances it's the 20th most-performed song by the classic line-up.

'Roger would wince when someone suggested 'Sheer Heart Attack' as an extra encore,' Brian May wrote in 2003. 'It was totally draining for him to keep up that pattern, especially when we got into it and it got more and more extended in our enthusiasm.' [17]

An original rough mix was released on the 2017 re-issue of *News of the World*. This is much more 'in your face', but without lead vocals.

'All Dead, All Dead' (Brian May)
May's first self-sung piano ballad. It's full of craft, as you would expect, and has some glorious guitar harmonies, but isn't particularly memorable. Freddie might have sung it better. The original rough mix was released on the 2017 re-issue of *News of the World*

'Spread Your Wings' (John Deacon)
Released as a single a-side, 10 February 1978 (UK), b/w 'Sheer Heart Attack'. UK: 34. Released as a single b-side (UK), 25 February 1996, b/w 'Too Much Love Will Kill You'.

The memorable, melodramatic 'Spread Your Wings' was John Deacon's second single as composer. Sung with real conviction by Freddie Mercury, it's the only Queen single without backing vocals stacked behind the powerful lead. It's a commercial song with a terrific chorus, and is a rare example of a simple, direct Queen lyric written in the third person – Sammy the bartender at The Emerald Bar dreams of a better life. 'Since he was small / Had no luck at all / Nothing came easy to him / Now it was time / He'd made up his mind / 'This could be my last chance''. It's a long way from 'The Fairy Feller's Master-Stroke'.

'Spread Your Wings reached only number 34 in the UK singles chart, and therefore wasn't included on *Greatest Hits* which is a great pity. The promotion film, recorded on a snowy day in Roger Taylor's back garden, is hilarious. Freddie wears his roadie's gloves as Brian May's hands get noticeably bluer.

'Spread Your Wings' was performed live from 1977 to 1981, and later with Adam Lambert who really gets under the skin of this song.

The single edit removes around forty seconds from the end of the song with an early fade. An alternative take and an instrumental version can be heard on the 2017 re-issue of *News of the World*. 'Spread Your Wings' was recorded for the BBC on 28 October 1977, the week that *News of the Word* came out. This version is on *On Air* and on the 2011 and 2017 re-issues of *News of the World*. It's faster and much longer than the studio version, with a more elaborate arrangement.

'Fight from the Inside' (Roger Taylor)

Roger Taylor sings and plays everything here except some of the lead guitar. The song is little more than a variation of riffs around the chords of D and A. But, as a contrast to the often over-arranged songs of Mercury and May, 'Fight from the Inside', noisy and imprudent, sits happily in the *News of the World* running order.

An instrumental version and 'demo vocal version' – essentially the released version with a different lead vocal take – were released on the 2017 re-issue of *News of the World*. The instrumental version has previously been released as part of *The eYe* video game.

'Get Down Make Love' (Freddie Mercury)

A simple, tense, rocking, sexy song full of passion and heat. The chorus-verse-bridge structure is split by a 'Whole Lotta Love' style interlude with squealing harmoniser and pumping drums.

Darryl Smyers writes: "Get Down, Make Love' is offensive in intent and execution. The song is the equivalent of 1970s porn done badly. The lyrics are the worst Mercury ever, ahem, came up with and that's saying something.' [18]

A filthy, dirty, and utterly brilliant song.
Robert Ham, Radio.com, November 2014

The final master consists of double-tracked bass guitar; seven tracks of drum kit; asymmetrical piano (recorded in stereo); three tracks of heavily distorted, feedback laden lead guitar; percussive sound effects (0:36); low and high harmony backing vocals (the 'every time I get high' sections ... all Freddie); a second vocal track over-dubbed four times in the central section (1:36-2:15); orgasmic sighs and shouts (2:40-3:10); and three tracks of that harmonised Red Special (2:34-3:10).

'Get Down, Make Love' was a set regular from 1977 to 1982. It was also performed by Queen + Adam Lambert in 2017-2018.

An early take and an instrumental version were both included on the 2017 re-issue of *News of the World*. A different instrumental version was released as part of *The eYe* video game. Some samples from the Queen version are included in Nine Inch Nails' terrific cover from 1990, released on the CD single 'Sin'.

'Sleeping on the Sidewalk' (Brian May)

A lifeless Cream-inspired rock-blues, written and sung by Brian May. If it sounds like a first take with the tape running, that's because it was. Performed on the *News of the World* tour in 1977, sung by Freddie Mercury who adds his own twist to the melody.

'Who Needs You?' (John Deacon)

A cute song with a Latino feel, with composer John Deacon playing nylon-strung Spanish guitar in addition to his usual bass guitar. Completed with a full band arrangement, with some lovely warm guitar fills from Brian May, the deceptive, laid-back performance hides the bitterness of the lyrics: 'I'm a fool for I believed your lies / But now I've seen through your disguise / Who needs, well I don't need, who needs you?'

'Who Needs You' may not be classic Queen – it's more of an interesting experiment – but it provides proof of John Deacon's expanding ambitions. The song is surely a blueprint for 'Feel the Pain' by George Michael.

An acoustic version was released on the 2017 re-issue of *News of the World*. This is an early take of the backing track, with guide vocal, before addition of bass, drums and electric guitar. The 'How I was pushed around…' section has not yet been written.

'It's Late' (Brian May)

Released as a single, 25 April 1978 (US), b/w 'Sheer Heart Attack'. 74.
'It's Late' is one of those epic Queen masterpieces that have been forgotten amongst the hit singles and endless compilations. Mercury's vocal delivery is astonishing – you believe every word he sings.

The intro is a slowed down, distorted variant of 'All Right Now' by Free (or perhaps 'Jessica' by the Allman Brothers Band) – this same riff is used in 'We Will Rock You' and 'Hammer to Fall'. The guitar solo includes one of the first widely available examples of the tapping technique made famous by Eddie Van Halen on the *Van Halen* album released the following year and arguably first heard on 'Dancing with the Moonlit Knight' by Genesis (1973). Freddie Mercury hits an unbelievable high note just as the final chorus kicks in.

'It's Late' was performed on the second half of the *News of the World* tour in 1978, and on the *Jazz* tour in 1978-1979. Adam Lambert treated the song with due reverence and his performances in 2017 were particularly good.

In its December 1977 review, the Washington Post would say:

'It's Late', a plaintive rock song in typical Queen style about a failed relationship. It is flawed by the instrumental break and high-powered instrumental ending, both of which go off on a drum and guitar bonanza, interrupting the otherwise neat structure and undercutting the melodic poignancy. And this seems to be a major problem with Queen: They don't

know when to end a song, they frequently succumb to excess in effects, and they tend to supply their songs with instrumental breaks that have little to do with anything.

An alternative version was released on the 2017 re-issue of *News of the World*. This sounds like a heavier mix – the band are very tight. It was also recorded for the BBC on 28 October 1977. This BBC version has a different solo section from the studio take and is available on both *On Air* and the 2017 re-issue of *News of the World*. The single version is heavily edited and is on the 2017 re-issue of *News of the World*. An instrumental version was released in 1996 as part of *The eYe*, a video game featuring music by Queen.

'My Melancholy Blues' (Freddie Mercury)

More of a jazz torch song than a twelve-bar, 'My Melancholy Blues' is a shuffling late-night cabaret lament with no guitars, no backing vocals and an extremely rare Mercury piano solo (2:13-2:41). It was performed on the *News of the World* tour, October 1977 to May 1978 as the third song in a short acoustic set with 'Love of My Life' and "39'.

A rough mix is available on the 2017 re-issue of *News of the World*. This sounds identical to the released mix to my ears. The song was also recorded for the BBC in October 1977 and released on *On Air* and on the 2011 and 2017 re-issues of *News of the World*

Other contemporary tracks
'Feelings, Feelings'

A studio gem, unreleased for forty years. Take 9 was widely available on bootleg, take 10 from July 1977 is available on the 2017 re-issue of *News of the World*. It's a short, rowdy, spirited rocker.

'Batteries Not Included'

Rumoured to be from the *News of the World* sessions, but unproven.

Jazz (1978)

Personnel:
Freddie Mercury: lead vocals, backing vocals, piano
Brian May: electric guitar, acoustic guitar, lead vocals, backing vocals
Roger Taylor: drums, lead vocals, backing vocals, percussion, electric guitar, bass guitar
John Deacon: bass guitar, electric guitar, acoustic guitar.
Recorded in July 1978 at Super Bear Studios, Berre-les-Alpes; July and August 1978 at Mountain Studios, Montreux; September and October 1978 at Super Bear Studios, Berre-les-Alpes. Produced by Queen and Roy Thomas Baker.
UK release date: 10 November 1978. US release date: 14 November 1978.
Highest chart places: UK: 2, USA: 6.

Queen's fractured, musically-diverse seventh album was their first to be recorded outside the UK, necessitated by punitive taxation of the band's new-found massive wealth. Sessions began at Super Bear Studios, a residential recording studio near Nice, in July 1978. Super Bear gained a reputation for technical excellence and innovation in the late 1970s – Kate Bush recorded her second album *Lionheart* at Super Bear in between Queen's sessions in summer 1978, and much of Pink Floyd's *The Wall* was recorded there in 1979. Work soon transferred to Mountain Studios in Montreux, Queen's first sessions at the studio they would buy the following year. Queen would record some or all of the albums *Hot Space* (1982), *A Kind of Magic* (1986), *The Miracle* (1989), *Innuendo* (1991) and *Made in Heaven* (1995) at Mountain, as well as most of their solo albums between 1981 and 1992. Other artists who recorded at Mountain during this period include AC/DC, David Bowie, Magnum, Iggy Pop and Chris Rea.

> *Queen's seventh album always splits the room. Some see Jazz as an underrated oddity: others as a confused, reactionary record that ... saw Queen's first dip in quality control. The truth lies somewhere in between.*
> James McNair, Q magazine, 2005

The chief engineer at Mountain was David Richards, a key collaborator for the final four Queen albums, which he both engineered and co-produced. The band returned to Super Bear to record vocals, final overdubs and to mix the album. For the first time, the songs on a Queen album are of a 'standard' length – all around three or four minutes. There are no lengthy epics or clever vignettes here.

'Jazz is full of energy and high spirits, incorporating a broad range of musical genres and a partial return to the big vocal arrangements of their earlier recordings,' notes Phil Chapman in *The Dead Straight Guide to Queen* (2017).

'Mustapha' (Freddie Mercury)
Arabic chants and scales are not your standard rock fare. But then, Queen were not your average rock band. The song ends with a multi-tracked wall of voices.

'Mustapha' was played in full in 1980 and sometimes in 1981. Freddie would occasionally improvise part of the song in one of his vocal extemporisations on subsequent tours. An edited version, just the introductory chant, was released as part of *The eYe* video game.

'Fat Bottomed Girls' (Brian May)
Single mix released as a single double a-side, 13 October 1978, b/w 'Bicycle Race'. UK 11. US: 24. Released on *Greatest Hits,* 1981. Released on the UK CD single for 'The Show Must Go On', 14 October 1991. UK: 16.

'Fat Bottomed Girls' is one of Brian May's simplest songs, mostly in D but with some cunning Fm ('fat bottomed GIRLS') and Em ('rockING world') chords to spice things up.

The song starts with a glorious *a capella* chorus – as does its flipside 'Bicycle Race' and the single mix of 'I Want It All'. Oh, and 'Bohemian Rhapsody'. The music for the verse is basic and almost brutal. The churning low-end bass sound was achieved by applying the drop D tuning to guitars and bass. On the album version rhythm guitar enters at 0:22, then second rhythm guitar and simplistic drums (from 0:35), handclaps (at 1:25) and double-tracked bass guitar (from 1:31).

The sound fills out for the second verse, and then we have that multi-layered chorus vocal and a powerful third verse with tom-tom fills and more overdubbed guitars (it sounds like overdubbed slide guitar *and* lead guitar from 2:32-2:53) and for a very full sound.

The last section includes some classic vocal asides from Freddie – 'get on your bikes and ride!', and 'ride 'em cowboy!' – and (on the album) the song has a triple shot hard ending giving the track a very live feel.

'Fat Bottomed Girls' was performed live from 1978 to 1982, and on later tours with Paul Rodgers and Adam Lambert.

The single version, also released on the 2011 re-issue of *Jazz*, has a less cluttered mix, chops out fifteen seconds at 0:21, another twenty-three at 1:08 and fades about twenty seconds early. A remix released on the 1991 re-issue of *Jazz* includes parts of a different vocal take at the end ('them dirty ladies get me every time!')

'Jealousy' (Freddie Mercury)
Released as a single a-side, 27 April 1979 (US), b/w 'Fun It'.

A beautiful, overlooked piano-driven mid-paced ballad with a skipping, melodic bass line. The sound and arrangement hark back to *Sheer Heart Attack*. Such was Queen's strength in depth that this song could have been a big hit for anyone else.

A remix, restoring Taylor's bass drum part, was released on *Deep Cuts, Volume 2* in 2011. This same remix was used on the 2011 remaster of *Jazz*, replacing the original mix from 1978.

'Bicycle Race' (Freddie Mercury)
Released as a single double a-side, 13 October 1978, b/w 'Fat Bottomed Girls'. UK 11. US: 24. Released on *Greatest Hits*, 1981.

The Tour de France passed through Montreux in mid-July 1978. Freddie wrote this utterly ridiculous song in response, recorded on Brian May's 31st birthday.

'Bicycle Race' is power pop-progressive in feel with a five-part harmony a chorus, a tense funk touch in the verses, anthemic rock in the bridge and multiple bicycle bells before the hard rocking guitar solo. What should sound disjointed and confusing is uplifting, joyous and a racing success. 'Bicycle Race' is surely one of the most intricate and rhythmically misleading top 20 hits.

It's an example of how a gifted songwriter can stitch together different keys, meters, tempos and styles and still be naturally commercial. The choruses are in A flat major, verses in B flat minor, the bridge in F major, the solo section is in D major. Both the third chorus and the bridge end in the key of C major. Five different keys in a hit song is most likely unique.

0:00 The powerful chorus opens the song, as it does with its flip-side, 'Fat Bottomed Girls'. Five-part vocal harmonies mixed into stereo are joined by piano, then drums, bass and guitar. There are hints of 'The March of the Black Queen' here.

0:22 A tight, funky verse, similar to 'Get Down, Make Love' but with call-and-response lyrics – some rhyming creatively ('white'/ 'bite', 'Royce'/ 'choice', 'Peter Pan'/ 'Superman') some not. There are off-beat accents from the piano, bass and drums which sound simple but try counting along.

0:40 The second chorus with Taylor working his hi-hat. Freddie's piano playing here is superlative.

1:00 The song swoops down to the bridge in a lower key, the meter changes to waltz time, we head four-part vocal harmonies with a nod to the song's double A-side ('bicycle races are coming your way / so forget all your duties, oh yeah / fat bottomed girls they'll be riding today / so look out for those beauties oh yeah'), guitar trills and 'on your marks, get set, go!'

1:31 A repeat of the first half of the chorus with gradual deceleration before the song halts completely.

1:45 This unforgettable section – and no doubt one where many non-Queen fans roll their eyes – has a series of jangling bicycle bells. This being Queen, they (more or less) build a harmonic chord. As they enter the bells sound the notes of A, D, F, E, A flat, C and G: a Dsus4 chord. 'Every bike shop in the area was scoured in order to build a collection of various tones of bell,' noted Freddie's roadie Peter 'Ratty' Hince. [19]

1:59 A melodic guitar solo starting with four tense, thrilling hammers-on. May's solo, driven by Mercury's energetic piano, then chases itself around the stereo spectrum.

2:16 The third verse with its Dylanesque interior rhyme of 'cheese', 'please' and 'Jesus' and the delightful rhythmic staccato conclusion of 'I don't wanna be a candidate / For Vietnam or Watergate…'.

2:34 The final chorus. A gradual decrease of speed towards the end gives the impression of bicycles rolling to a stop at almost exactly three minutes.

'Bicycle Race' was performed live by Queen in 1978-1979, usually as part of a medley, and by Queen + Adam Lambert in 2017.

A pointless hip-hop remix with most of the instrumentation replaced by back-beats and loops was released on the 1991 re-issue of *Jazz*. It's all very well done, but just who was this aimed at? The backing track was released on the 2011 re-issue of *Jazz* – this highlights the complex arrangement, especially Deacon's athletic bass playing.

Darryl Smyers of the *Dallas Observer* doesn't like it: 'A horrible mix of vaudeville-inspired rock and pretentious, a cappella nonsense, this song is a disgrace to two-wheelers everywhere.'

'If You Can't Beat Them' (John Deacon)

This seemingly simple crowd-pleasing rocker, with it's very basic D, A and G chords, hides a wry arrangement with some tricky changes, syncopations, stops and a half-step key change.

'Another selection for the guitar student's lesson book,' suggests Robert Ham, 'May solos for over two minutes and not one second feels wasted.' [1]

Think Cheap Trick with an electronics degree.

Performed on the first leg of the Jazz tour in 1978, and again in 1980 and 1981.

'Let Me Entertain You' (Freddie Mercury)

A live version recorded on the European tour of January to March 1979, was released as a single b-side in the US on 24 August 1979, b/w 'We Will Rock You' (fast version from *Live Killers*).

This is Freddie's last full-on arena-rocker until 'Prices of the Universe' in 1986. Although, Freddie being Freddie, the introduction and chorus are in shuffling waltz time, whilst the rest of the song is four-to-the-floor rock and roll.

Performed live from 1978 to 1981. An edited version, just the introduction, was released as part of *The eYe* video game.

'Dead on Time' (Brian May)

One of the two big rockers on *Jazz*, 'Dead on Time' is driven by a fast guitar riff reminiscent of 'Stone Cold Crazy' and a tricky drum part. There are references to 'Keep Yourself Alive' both musically (the riffed, phased guitar break) and lyrically ('Leave on time, leave on time / Got to keep yourself alive / Gotta leave on time'). The closing thunderbolt is 'courtesy of God', which is odd coming from an astrophysicist.

'In Only Seven Days' (John Deacon)

Released as a single b-side, 26 January 1979, b/w 'Don't Stop Me Now'.

This sweet ballad showcases both John Deacon's characteristic melodies and his romantic lyrics. It's very Paul McCartney. Deacon plays acoustic and electric guitar, as well as bass, and it sounds like Deacon playing the guitar solo as well. Mercury's piano-playing and singing is sublime. The final moments are the closest to jazz on *Jazz*, with Deacon's beautiful strummed acoustic guitar to the fore. Fact: this song is on the same album as 'Don't Stop Me Now' and 'Fat Bottomed Girls'.

'Dreamer's Ball' (Brian May)

A tribute to Elvis Presley, this shuffling slow blues has a boozy guitar-band arrangement similar to 'Good Company', and some very tight harmonies. The first guitar solo works around the vocal melody; the second is fully harmonised in classic Queen style.

Performed on the *Jazz* tour, 1978-1979.

An acoustic take, recorded August 1978, was released on the 2011 re-issue of *Jazz*. This sounds much jazzier, especially Taylor's brushed drums. Mercury's closely miked vocal is effortless.

'Fun It' (Roger Taylor)

Released as a single b-side, 27 April 1979 (US), b/w 'Jealousy'.

'Fun It' is another example of Roger Taylor adding significant variety of style to Queen's musical palette. It is an out-and-out funk track, economic in arrangement and delivery sung by Taylor (verses) and Mercury (choruses). It's surely a blueprint for 'Another One Bites the Dust', a pre-cursor to *Hot Space* and a companion to 'Rock It'. Presumably EMI didn't like 'Funk It' as a title.

Performed on the second leg of the *Jazz* tour, 1979.

'Leaving Home Ain't Easy' (Brian May)

'Leaving Home Ain't Easy' is a folky ballad with some beautiful three-part vocal harmonies. May's singing is uncertain – as a lead vocalist he's no Freddie Mercury; this would be the last time he would take sole credit as lead vocalist on a Queen studio album. The song is attractively arranged and performed, especially Deacon's bass in the chorus which perfectly underpins the vocals. The closely miked acoustic guitar with three-part bottleneck slide and careful volume control emulate the sound of a pedal-steel guitar and hark back to the California song-writer style of the Eagles, James Taylor and Jackson Browne, with a bit of progressive rock.

'Don't Stop Me Now' (Freddie Mercury)

Released as a single a-side, 26 January 1979, b/w 'In Only Seven Days'. UK: 9. US: 86. Released on *Greatest Hits*, 1981.

' A song that's full of joy and optimism.' Brian May, commentary on *Absolute Greatest*, 2009

'Don't Stop Me Now' must surely be one of Queen's greatest songs. This is Freddie Mercury through and through – the lines 'Don't stop me now / 'Cause I'm having such a good time' could easily be his epitaph. Written in the upbeat piano-based style of older songs such as 'Good Old-Fashioned Lover Boy' and 'Seaside Rendezvous', 'Don't Stop Me Now' is a life-affirming, I-don't-give-a-shit blast of unadulterated Freddie Mercury. His piano-playing is incendiary.

As with other songs on *Jazz*, what sounds simple and commercial includes many tricks of advanced song writing – uneven phrasing, syncopations, vocal harmonies and break-downs, and a mighty lead vocal with drive, slid notes, vibrato and falsetto. There's also an incisive and thrilling thirty-second guitar solo where not a single note is wasted. The alternative 'long lost guitars' version released in 2011 has a different guitar solo: May's final version was clearly the result of much work.

On previous albums, ideas such as these would be spread across longer songs such as 'The March of the Black Queen', 'Liar' or 'When the Night Comes'. With 'Don't Stop Me Now', this constantly inventive, breathless blast of adrenalin lasts just 3:29 and was a top ten hit in the UK.

The song was performed on the second leg of the *Jazz* tour in 1979 after its release a single, and in 1980 and 1981 and on tours with Adam Lambert. An alternative mix, with 'long lost guitars', was released on the 1991 re-issue of *Jazz*. This proves that the band got it right the first time as this mix sounds unduly cluttered.

'More of that Jazz' (Roger Taylor)
Hardly a typical album closer, with a heavy, churning arrangement, no doubt with tongue firmly in cheek. Only two of the band perform: we hear a terrific Roger Taylor vocal (his last as sole lead vocalist on a full Queen studio album) and many twisting Brian May riffs, until the unexpected cut-in of excerpts from other songs on the album to take us to the stop-go ending. Remarkable stuff.

Footnotes
[1] *Classic Albums*, 2005.
[2] *Classic Albums*, 2005.
[3] *Classic Albums*, 2005.
[4] Radio.com, November 2014.
[5] *Classic Albums*, 2005.
[6] commentary on *Absolute Greatest*, 2009. The clip is on YouTube at the time of writing. Go on, you know you want to!
[7] *Classic Albums*, 2005.
[8] *Classic Albums*, 2005.
[9] *Queen Unseen*, 2015.
[10] *Classic Albums*, 2005.
[11] The top 10 was 'The Lark Ascending' (Vaughan Williams), 'Enigma Variations' (Elgar), 'Symphony No. 9: Choral' (Beethoven), 'Bohemian Rhapsody' (Queen), 'Comfortably Numb' (Pink Floyd), 'Cello Concerto in E Minor' (Elgar), 'Messiah' (Handel), 'The Planets' (Holst), 'Fantasy on a Theme by Thomas Tallis' (Vaughan Williams), 'Requiem in D Minor' (Mozart).
[12] commentary on *Absolute Greatest*, 2009.
[13] *NME*, December 1976.
[14] *The Complete Guide to the Music of Queen*, 2006.
[15] *Queen Unseen*, 2015.

[16] commentary on *Absolute Greatest*, 2009.
[17] response to fan query, April 2003, published at brianmay.com.
[18] *Dallas Observer*, July 2014.
[19] *Queen Unseen*, 2015.

1979–1984: Staying Power

There's an argument that suggests that Queen's first seven albums were each written as cohesive wholes: collections of songs that worked together, that flowed and ebbed as albums should, and that any hit singles were due to serendipity and an ear for a catchy melody.

All of this changed in 1979. Suddenly Queen very much had an eye on the singles charts. If any point marks Queen's final transition from album-band-with-hit-singles to we're-a-singles-band-who-put-out-albums, then *The Game* is the place to look. Four singles were drawn from *The Game* and from each of their subsequent three albums. The idea of a consistent quality control throughout an album was seemingly discarded.

'For some long-serving fans,' wrote Peter Kane in 2005, 'this simpler direction was viewed almost as a breach of trust: a feeling compounded by Freddie's acquisition of a big, bushy, unofficially gay moustache.'

Queen's sound also changed: their 'no synths' rule was finally abandoned and the dance-floor rhythms of disco and funk were fully explored. The colossal hit 'Another One Bites the Dust' attracted many listeners to Queen for the first time. But some longer-term supporters regarded this as a sell-out. The seven years from 1979 saw Queen move to huge concert arenas and score a further fourteen UK top 20 hits, including four UK number ones, six number twos and three number threes.

For ten years, the songs that were not singles, with a few exceptions, were very often little more than well-crafted filler. It's this period that separates the long-term fans, there from the beginning (more or less) from those who thought that Queen's first album was called *Greatest Hits* – the best-selling album of all time in the UK.

By the time of *The Miracle* and *Innuendo*, recorded in 1988-1990, Queen had switched back to seeing an album as a single large statement.

The Game (1980)

Personnel:
Freddie Mercury: lead vocals, backing vocals, keyboards, acoustic guitar
Brian May: electric guitar, acoustic guitar, lead vocals, backing vocals, keyboards
Roger Taylor: drums, backing vocals, electric guitar, keyboards
John Deacon: bass guitar, electric guitar, acoustic guitar, keyboards
+ Reinhold Mack – keyboards on 'Rock It (Prime Jive').
Recorded June – July 1979 and February – May 1980 at Musicland Studios, Munich.
Produced by Queen and Mack.
UK release date: 30 June 1980. US release date: 1 July 1980.
Highest chart places: UK: 1, USA: 1.

Queen recorded *The Game* in two batches of sessions, at a new venue: Georgio Moroder's Musicland Studio in the basement of the Arabella Hotel in Munich.

Freddie Mercury would buy an apartment in Munich in 1983. Celebrated albums recorded at Musicland before Queen's arrival include *It's Only Rock and Roll* by the Rolling Stones (1973-1974), *Stormbringer* and *Come Taste the Band* by Deep Purple (1974 and 1975), *Presence* by Led Zeppelin (recorded late 1975), *Richie Blackmore's Rainbow* and *Rainbow Rising* (1975 and 1976) and *Calling Card* by Rory Gallagher (1976). The Electric Light Orchestra had recorded four albums there including their massively successful *Out of the Blue* recorded May to August 1977.

The studio's engineer, Reinhold Mack, would co-produce *The Game, Flash Gordon, Hot Space, The Works* and *A Kind of Magic*, giving a commercial sheen to Queen's mid-period work.

For the first time, the band broke their previous 'no synthesisers' rule. 'We had always been keen to try out anything new or different whilst recording,' *says* John Deacon in *As It Began*. 'The synthesisers then were so good, [they] could duplicate all sorts of sounds and instruments – you could get a whole orchestra out of them at the touch of button.'

The first sessions for *The Game*, in June and July 1979, resulted in the songs 'Coming Soon' and 'Sail Away Sweet Sister', and the huge hits 'Crazy Little Thing Called Love' (released October 1979) and 'Save Me' (January 1980). Queen returned to live performance in November and December 1979 then went back to Munich to complete the album from February to May 1980.

'Everything was different,' explained Brian May to *On the Record* in 1982. 'Mack had come from a different background from us. Mack's first contribution was to say, 'If it breaks down after half a minute, then we can edit in and carry on if you just play along with the tempo'. We laughed and said 'Don't be silly. You can't do that'. But in fact, you can. What you gain is the freshness, because often the backing track is first time though. It really helped a lot.'

The Game was the only Queen album to reach no. 1 in both the UK and the US. It was also their last big hit album in America: their subsequent seven releases reached no higher than no. 22 in the Billboard album charts.

'Play the Game' (Freddie Mercury)
Released as a single a-side, 30 May 1980, b/w 'A Human Body'. UK: 14. US: 42. Released on *Greatest Hits,* 1981.
The 'no synths' label from every album since *Queen II* is finally abandoned here – and how, as the opening track starts with a clever update of the introduction to 'Death on Two Legs' with swoops of thrilling, reversed synthesiser noises sucking the listener into the first verse.

'Play the Game' is a power ballad in the classic Queen style. Brian May's powerful guitar flourishes and John's Deacon's contrapuntal bass patterns provide the dynamics. But it is Freddie's percussive piano and splendid vocal that are at the heart of this wonderful song.

'Play the Game' was included in the band's live set between 1980 and 1982 and performed with Adam Lambert in 2016.

'Who wouldn't feel hopeful about their romantic prospects after hearing this fantastic ballad?' asks Robert Ham. 'The song also offers up plenty of chances to marvel at Freddie Mercury's vocal abilities. Don't believe me? You try singing it and see how well it goes.' [1]

'Dragon Attack' (Brian May)

Released as a single b-side, 22 August 1980, b/w 'Another One Bites the Dust'. 'Dragon Attack' is a slice of solid funk from Brian May, praising the distractions of Munich nightclubs such as the Sugar Shack. 'Take me to the room where the red's all red / Take me out of my head, 's what I said / Take me to the room where the green's all green / And from what I've seen it's hot, it's mean'

'We visit a disco very often,' said Roger Taylor at the time. 'The Sugar Shack is the hottest disco in the world.' [2]

With May's tight hard-rock guitar riffs heavily stopped in the verses and howling through the solo and Mercury's typically full throttle vocal, 'Dragon Attack' is stylistically the polar opposite of 'Keep Yourself Alive' from eight years and seven albums earlier. The song was added to the live set in August 1980, just after its release as the b-side to 'Another One Bites the Dust' and retained until 1985. For some of this time it was inserted into 'Now I'm Here'. It was also performed with Adam Lambert in 2012 and 2014 with a lengthy bass solo. [3]

A remix, released on the 1991 re-issue of *The Works*, reworked the track with a sampled backbeat lending a real urgency to the song. With almost all of May's guitars removed it doesn't much sound like Queen, and the rap section sounds contrived, but as a mash-up of rock and hip-hop styles it works surprisingly well. Released as an instrumental as part of *The eYe*.

'Another One Bites the Dust' (John Deacon)

Released as a single a-side, 22 August 1980, b/w 'Dragon Attack'. UK: 7. US: 1. Released on *Greatest Hits*, 1981.

John Deacon started work on 'Another One Bites the Dust' in autumn 1979, between the two sets of sessions for *The Game*. Surely the band's nightly visits to Munich clubs had more than a passing influence, as did the New York funk/disco band Chic who had scored four UK top ten hits in 1977-1978, the most obvious precedent being 'Good Times', released in June 1979. In an interview with *NME*, Chic co-founder Bernard Edwards stated, 'That Queen record came about because that Queen bass player ... spent some time hanging out with us at our studio.'

'Good Times' was recorded in the early part of 1979 at the Power Station in New York and released on 30 June. Deacon was on tour in Europe between mid-January and early March 1979, and in Asia between mid-April and mid May 1979. So, if he really did visit Chic in New York then it must have been in March or April, or possibly late May. Certainly, the intervals and low E 'dum-dum-dum-[rest]-da-dum-dum' bass notes of the first half of each repeated bar are identical in both 'Good Times' and 'Another One Bites the Dust'.

The final version features Deacon's keyboards, handclaps and sprightly Chic-style electric rhythm guitar in the choruses (with palm-muted doubling of the bass in the verses). Roger Taylor added a heavily echoed drum loop, Brian May contributes stereo sound effects with guitar and harmoniser and Freddie Mercury provides one of his most energetic vocals with many glissandos, breathy sighs and improvised grunts. He is double- and triple-tracked in the chorus and self-harmonises most of the final verse. The swoop into falsetto in the 'Are you happy, are you satisfied? / How long can you stand the heat? / Out of the doorway the bullets rip / To the sound of the beat' is effortlessly controlled. Deacon, of course, plays that simple, strong and funky-as-fuck bass line.

A remarkable interlude (1:40 to 2:28) drops out all instrumentation except the rhythm loop, building up with handclaps (1:46), guitar effects (1:49-1:58), guitar-with-harmoniser (1:58-2:06), reversed piano (2:06-2:12), percussion (2:12-2:16) and then just the title phrase repeated four times with different endings each time ('ah!', 'ow!', 'hey hey!' and 'hey-ay-ay!', 2:20-2:28). The level of invention here is extraordinary.

In the early 1980s, 'Another One Bites the Dust' was one of many songs that was alleged to contain subliminal messages via backwards masking. The chorus, when played in reverse, can be heard as 'decide to smoke marijuana', 'it's fun to smoke marijuana', or 'start to smoke marijuana'. Nonsense.

The song garnered a Grammy Award nomination in 1981 for Best Rock Performance by a Duo or Group with Vocal. The video also saw the debut of Mercury's moustache.

'Another One Bites the Dust' was not initially intended as a single – legend has it that Michael Jackson urged them to release it after attending a Queen concert in Inglewood in July 1980. 'We weren't going to release this as a single,' said Roger Taylor in 2009. 'It was Michael Jackson's suggestion. I thought he was nuts.'

'Another One Bites the Dust' was added to the live set in August 1980, six weeks into their tour to promote *The Game*. A perennial at every Queen concert thereafter, it was also performed with Paul Rodgers, where much of the energy was lost, and with Adam Lambert where he came close to Mercury's power and delivery.

A remix called 'Another One Bites the Dust (Long Dusted B-Boy Mix)' was released on a sampler CD in 1992 on the Hollywood BASIC label. Nearly eleven minutes long, this excellent mix strips down 'Another One Bites the Dust' adding samples of 'The Breaks' by Kurtis Blow, 'Apache' by the Sugarhill Gang, 'It's More Fun to Compute' by Kraftwerk, 'Good Times' by Chic (naturally) and many others. 'Another One Bites the Dust (Small Soldiers album version)' was released 14 November 1998 credited to Queen + Wyclef Jean featuring Pras and Free. UK: 5. Also released on *Greatest Hits III*. This is a remix by Wyclef Jean of the Fugees, with additional raps by Pras and Free. There are also the 'Another One Bites the Dust (Team 1 Black Rock Star Main Pass Mix)' and 'Another One Bites the Dust (Team 1 Black Rock Star Radio Edit)' also credited to Queen + Wyclef Jean featuring Pras and Free. These remixes are both closer to the original track. Instrumental and *a capella* versions were released on a promo CD. The track was re-mixed with new vocals in 2003, credited to Queen + Annie Crummer, from the Australian release of the *We Will Rock You* cast album tenth anniversary re-issue and on the *We Will Rock You - Around the World* EP. There are also several remixes credited to Queen vs. The Miami Project: 'Another One Bites the Dust (Cedric Gervais & Second Sun Radio Edit)', CD single. UK: 31. The CD single also includes 'Another One Bites the Dust (Cedric Gervais & Second Sun Vocal Mix)', 'Another One Bites the Dust (Oliver Koletzki Remix)', 'Another One Bites the Dust (A Skillz Remix)', 'Another One Bites the Dust (Soul Avengerz Remix)' and 'Another One Bites the Dust (DJ Pedro & Olivier Berger Mix)'. A further mix, 'Another One Bites the Dust (Soul Avengerz Dub)', was available as a download.

'Need Your Loving Tonight' (John Deacon)
Released as a single in the US, 18 November 1980, b/w 'Rock It (Prime Jive)'. US: 44.
This punchy power pop song suggests the influence of The Beatles – favourites of all of the band – mixed with the sensibilities of recent hits by the likes of Cheap Trick ('Surrender', June 1978), Blondie ('Hanging on the Telephone', August 1978) and The Knack ('My Sharona', June 1979).

Performed frequently in summer 1980, then less frequently in winter 1980, hardly at all in 1981 and never thereafter.

'Crazy Little Thing Called Love' (Freddie Mercury)
Released as a single a-side, 5 October 1979, b/w 'We Will Rock You' (fast version from *Live Killers*). UK 2. US: 1. Released on *Greatest Hits,* 1981.
Queen's retro-boogie rockabilly juggernaut was the first song recorded for *The Game*, during the first batch of sessions in June and July 1979. The song was written by Freddie Mercury in the bath in his room at the Bayerischer Hof Hotel in Munich

> Crazy Little Thing Called Love' took me five or ten minutes. I did that on the guitar, which I can't play for nuts, and in one way it was quite a good thing because I was restricted, knowing only a few chords. It's a good discipline because I simply had to write within a small framework. I couldn't work through too many chords and because of that restriction I wrote a good song, I think.
> Freddie Mercury, *Melody Maker*, May 1981

'Fred wanted to take a bath before going to the studio,' notes Peter Hince. '[He] was humming and tapping … and shouting out the names of chords: 'D – yes, and C and G. Ratty! Quick! Get me a guitar now!' I gave him the acoustic that had been installed for these impulsive creative moments. Fred strummed away for a short time [and] we dashed to Musicland where a halt was called to whatever work was in progress. They started to record [this new idea] immediately.' [4]

The bulk of the backing track was completed in a single session: a testament to the simplicity of the arrangement, necessitated by Mercury's self-confessed lack of ability on guitar, and as a tribute to the rock and roll sound of the 1950s. The finished master comprises bass, heavily compressed drums (mostly hi-hat, kick and snare with rim shots), lead vocals, backing vocals, acoustic guitar, lead guitar and handclaps, all massively echoed in stereo for that '50s Sun Studios sound.

Released as a single, six months ahead of the album, 'Crazy Little Thing Called Love' was the band's first statement as a singles-led band and topped the US billboard charts for four weeks in February and March 1980.

The song was performed at every Queen concert from November 1979 onwards, and on the tours with Paul Rodgers and Adam Lambert. In 1970s-1980s concerts, May would play the guitar solo on a Fender Telecaster before switching back to his Red Special for the conclusion. The live arrangement would end with a few chords from 'You're My Best Friend'. Performances with Paul Rodgers' would add an effective bluesy swagger to the song.

'Rock It (Prime Jive)' (Roger Taylor)

Released as a single b-side, 18 November 1980 (US), b/w 'Need Your Loving Tonight'. US: 44.

'Rock It (Prime Jive)' starts as a slow, very basic soul ballad in 6/8 – shades of Otis Redding's 'These Arms of Mine' and the band's own 'Tenement Funster' – before kicking off as a pulsing power pop song with a tense guitar solo. A companion to 'Fun It'.

'Rock It (Prime Jive)' was included in the set a few times in 1980, then frequently (around 40 times) in 1981, usually as the set opener.

'Don't Try Suicide (Nobody Gives a Damn)' (Freddie Mercury)

An economically-arranged song, with a blues feel in the verses, four-square rock in the chorus and rockabilly in the bridge and solo. The introduction and verses owe much to the Police song 'Walking on the Moon', released in November 1979 and, co-incidentally, written in Munich.

The lyrics are uncharacteristically shallow for Freddie Mercury – 'So you think it's the easy way out / Think you're gonna slash your wrists / This time baby when you do it / All you do is get on my tits.' The subject matter is David Minns who Freddie had dumped in spring 1977 and had taken an overdose in response. 'He wrote that song ... in my honour,' wrote Minns in 1993.

'How sweet of him. The acid queen had finally shown his true colours.' [5]

'Sail Away Sweet Sister' (Brian May)

A lovely rock ballad recorded during the first batch of sessions for *The Game* in early summer 1979. One of the few songs from *The Game* to hark back to earlier Queen albums – this could easily come from *A Night at the Opera* – 'Sail Away Sweet Sister' has reflective, mostly acoustic verses with choruses driven by electric guitar. It is mostly sung by Brian May. Freddie Mercury's quite awesome vocal interlude ('Hot child don't you know you're young / You got your whole life ahead of you? / And you can throw it away too soon / Way too soon') merely shows how weak May's lead vocals could be when not backed up by other voices. 'Sail Away Sweet Sister' might have been one of Queen's very best songs if Mercury had sung throughout.

'I got Freddie to learn [the piano part] and play it with Roger and John for the backing track,' writes Brian May, 'I wanted his marvellous rhythm and percussive feel on piano.' [6]

This song is a refreshing antidote to often overblown and lush arrangements elsewhere. Take one with guide vocal was released on the 2011 re-issue of *The Game*. This is a work-in-progress with vocals throughout by Brian May.

Robert Ham: 'Heartbreak rarely sounds this buoyant and rocking.' [7]

'Coming Soon' (Roger Taylor)

Recorded during the first batch of sessions for *The Game* in June and July 1979. 'Coming Soon' is a companion piece to 'Need Your Loving Tonight', Cars-style power pop with a hint of glam rock in its pounding drums. It's filler – high class filler, but filler just the same.

'Save Me' (Brian May)

A single mix, with additional phasing, a different guitar sound and some percussion mixed lower was released as a single a-side, 25 January 1980, b/w 'Let Me Entertain You'. UK: 11. Also available on *Greatest Hits*, 1981.

'Save Me' is one of those classic Queen songs that seems to give everything you'd expect from this band – ballad verses with a stark lyric, an anthemic uplifting chorus, a fat rhythm section, layers of acoustic guitars, a powerful bass line, harmony guitars, a tight, passionate guitar solo, layered harmony vocals and, best of all, a lead vocal from Freddie Mercury that ranges from a tender serenade to full-tilt power. 'The years of care and loyalty / Were nothing but a sham it seems / The years belie we lived a lie / I love you till I die'.

Mercury's five-note ornament on 'alone' (3:49) is worth the price of admission itself.

Recorded during the first batch of sessions for *The Game* in June and July 1979 'Save Me' was released as a single six months ahead of the album. The partially-animated promo film is one of their best. 'Save Me' was performed in concert between 1979 and 1982. The band's live arrangement was very effective: Brian May would play piano for the first verse, first chorus and second verse, then switch to guitar – Freddie would take over piano for the solo sections and final chorus, giving a very full sound. The song was also performed with Adam Lambert in 2014-2015 and 2017.

Other contemporary songs

'A Human Body'
Released as a single b-side, 30 May 1980, b/w 'Play the Game' and on the 2011 re-issue of *The Game*. This is a folky ballad written and sung by Roger Taylor, shows many of his key song writing traits: guitar arpeggios ('Tenement Funster'), waltz time ('I'm In Love with My Car', 'Drowse', 'Coming Soon') and vocoder (the forthcoming 'Radio Ga Ga').

'Sandbox'
A fun song, powered by Freddie's piano – authoritative and tight, with lots of lots of potential but seemingly never finished.

'It's a Beautiful Day'
A short demo recorded in April 1980 during sessions for *The Game*. Freddie sings and accompanies himself on piano. It was reworked by the surviving band members, to great effect, for *Made in Heaven*. This utterly sublime unadorned piano/vocal take is included on the 2011 re-release of *The Game*, April 1980.

Flash Gordon (1980)
Personnel:
Freddie Mercury: lead and backing vocals, synthesisers, piano and other keyboards
Brian May: electric guitar, lead vocals, backing vocals, synthesisers, piano, organ
Roger Taylor: drums, timpani, synthesisers, backing vocals
John Deacon: bass, guitar, synthesisers.
Recorded between mid-February and March 1980 at The Town House, and October-November 1980 at The Town House, the Music Centre, and Advision Studios, London. [8] Produced by Queen and Mack.
UK release date: 8 December 1980. US release date: 27 January 1981.
Highest chart places: UK: 10, USA: 23.

1979-1980 was a very busy period for Queen: a European tour between January and March 1979; mixing *Live Killers* in March 1979; dates in Japan in April-May 1979; recording sessions for *The Game* in June and July 1979; a UK tour in November-December 1979; sessions for *The Game* from February to May 1980; a North American tour from June to September 1980; another European tour in November and December 1980.

Amongst all this activity, which gave them two number one singles in the US, Queen agreed to write and record the soundtrack to the very cheesy $22 million comic-strip sci-fi film *Flash Gordon*. The film was directed by Mike Hodges, produced by Dino De Laurentiis and had an international cast including Max Von Sydow, Peter Wyngarde, Timothy Dalton, Topol and Brian Blessed.

It was interesting to see how [the band] approached what was a creative 'carte blanche' with no strict format to follow. They were not being asked to produce 'songs' with verses, choruses and a middle eight. As a musician it must have been fulfilling to use the inspiration from the visuals in the film and match it with your own musical input to create mood and drama.

Peter 'Ratty' Hince, *Queen Unseen*, 2015

Out of necessity, Queen's work for *Flash Gordon* was pieced together in and around their busy schedule, mostly by Brian May who shares production credits with Mack. Queen's distinctive sound threads through the album and film, although with just two songs and sixteen short instrumental pieces, many fans were left short-changed. An alternative mix of the title track was a top ten hit in Austria, Germany, Ireland and the UK.

'Flash's Theme' (Brian May)

Released as a single a-side, renamed simply 'Flash', on 24 November 1980, b/w 'Football Fight'. UK: 10. US: 42. Also available on *Greatest Hits,* and the 1991 and 2011 re-releases of *Flash Gordon.*

This is the film's opening music, much more familiar in its single remix than in the album version. It's a wonderful exercise in dynamic camp – the pulsing piano pushes the tension and we achieve release through the flashes of harmony vocals ('ah-aaaaa!') and falsetto ('He'll save with a mighty hand / Every man, every woman, every child, with a mighty flash').

The single, Queen's 19th but Brian May's first top ten hit as a writer, includes more dialogue from the film including the immortal lines 'Flash, I love you, but we have only fourteen hours to save the earth!' and 'Gordon's alive!'.

Added to the live set in early December 1980 to coincide with its release as a single, 'Flash's Theme' was performed through to the end of the 1982 tour dates. As with 'Save Me' Brian May would play piano during the first half of the song, and guitar in the second. It was also used as intro music by Queen + Adam Lambert in 2012 and 2016.

A remix on the 1991 re-issue of *Flash Gordon* is almost seven minutes long with looped backbeats and repeated vocal samples. It's tedious. Queen + Vanguard released 'Flash (Vanguard Mix)' and 'Flash (Radio Mix)' in 2003. They are very tedious. The 12' single added 'Flash (Extended Mix)', 'Flash (Electro Mix)', 'Flash (Tomcraft Mix)' and 'Flash (Christian Smith & John Selway Mix)'. Yay.

'Football Fight' (Freddie Mercury)

Released as a single b-side, 24 November 1980, b/w 'Flash'.

A furious, synth-driven instrumental full of Mercury dynamics and power, used for one of the fight scenes in the film. An alternative version from February 1980 ('early version – no synths') is an exhilarating piano-driven piece which would have formed the basis for a great song. This is available on the 2011 re-

release of *Flash Gordon*.

'Ming's Theme (In the Court of Ming the Merciless)', 'The Ring (Hypnotic Seduction of Dale)', 'Vultan's Theme (Attack of the Hawk Men)' (Freddie Mercury)

Both the short, discordant 'The Ring' and the unsettling 'Ming's Theme' are performed by Freddie Mercury on keyboards, the latter with Roger Taylor (percussion) and Howard Blake's orchestra. The furious, pulsating Wagner-on-synths 'Vultan's Theme' is one of the first Queen songs to have a synth bass part: this would be a common Queen sound in the 1980s. It was performed live in 1981 as part of a *Flash Gordon* medley.

'In the Space Capsule (The Love Theme)', 'In the Death Cell (Love Theme Reprise)', 'Escape from the Swamp' (Roger Taylor)

Three pieces written and mostly performed by Roger Taylor: all guitars on 'In the Space Capsule (The Love Theme)' are by Taylor, and probably all keyboards as well. 'In the Death Cell' is a variation of 'In the Space Capsule' and 'Escape from the Swamp' is mostly tuned timpani and phasing synthesisers. These three pieces are particularly effective in the context of the film. None were performed live by Queen.

'Execution of Flash', 'Arboria (Planet of the Tree Men)' (John Deacon)

Deacon's asymmetrical Fender Stratocaster guitar part in the stark 'Execution of Flash' is accompanied by orchestra and bells. 'Arboria (Planet of the Tree Men)' is a bleakly effective ambient track featuring just synthesiser.

'The Kiss (Aura Resurrects Flash)' (Freddie Mercury and Howard Blake)

The symphonic, atmospheric 'The Kiss' comprises Freddie's synthesiser and multi-tracked vocals with Howards Blake's orchestral score developed from Freddie's vocal improvisations. It's quite the best thing on this album. An even better version from March 1980, just piano and vocals, is available on the 2011 re-release of *Flash Gordon*.

'I remember Freddie Mercury singing … in his high falsetto and I showed him how I could expand it into the orchestral section now on the film, with which he seemed very pleased,' writes Howard Blake at howardblake.com.

'Flash to the Rescue', 'Battle Theme', 'Crash Dive on Mingo City', 'Flash's Theme Reprise (Victory Celebrations)' (Brian May)

'Flash to the Rescue' is a development and variant of 'Flash's Theme' with

76

the same pulsating piano, bass guitar and bass drum, and many of the same dialogue excerpts and sound effects used on the single mix. 'Battle Theme' is a loud, extravagant guitar-driven piece developed from the central section of 'Flash's Theme'. Intriguingly, Vultan (Brian Blessed) is heard shouting 'who wants to live forever?' in one of the dialogue samples from the film. 'Battle Theme' was performed live in 1981 as part of a *Flash Gordon* medley. The minute-long 'Crash Dive on Mingo City' comprises heavily stopped power chords and loud drums. 'Flash's Theme Reprise (Victory Celebrations)' is the 'he'll save every one of us' section from 'Flash's Theme', with stirring dialogue from Timothy Dalton, Topol and Melody Anderson.

'The Wedding March' (Richard Wagner, arranged by Brian May)
Multiple harmonic guitars and crashing drums colour this unmistakable Queen version of Wagner's 'Bridal Chorus' from the opera *Lohengrin*.

'Marriage of Dale and Ming (And Flash Approaching)' (Brian May and Roger Taylor)
Another pieced based around 'Flash's Theme', but with elements of 'Love Theme', hence the joint writing credit.

> *Minister: 'Do you, Ming the Merciless, Ruler of the Universe, take this Earthling Dale Arden to be your empress of the hour? Do you promise to use her as you will and not to blast her into space until such time you grow weary of her?'*
> *Ming: 'I do.'*
> *Dale: 'I do not!'*

'The Hero' (Brian May and Howard Blake)
A hard-rocking track played over the final credits of the film – it's a development of 'Battle Theme' and sounds like classic early-'70s Queen songs such as 'Seven Seas of Rhye' and 'Keep Yourself Alive'. It neatly integrates a reprise of 'Flash's Theme' into its arrangement.

> *Brian May came over one day and hummed an idea. As he did so I jotted it down on some manuscript paper and then played it back on the piano, which really startled him. They all came along to the orchestral recordings and seemed fascinated. Whilst scoring I had cassettes of guitar ideas from Brian. I wrote this out into my score at one point and surrounded it with big orchestral colour. When I came to the recording I had Brian's solo guitar on headphones and conducted the orchestra in synch around it.*
> Howard Blake at howardblake.com

'The Hero' was added to the band's setlist in November 1980 and performed on most of the dates through to spring 1981. It was performed sporadically in late 1981, and then used to open live shows on the European leg of the *Hot Space* tour in 1982. It was also performed by Queen + Adam Lambert in 2012 (brief excerpt) and 2016 (full song).

An excellent version called 'October 1980 ... revisited' is available on the 2011 re-release of *Flash Gordon*. This is a powerful guitar-heavy remix of the album version featuring a double-tracked lead vocal from Freddie.

Hot Space (1981)

Personnel:
Freddie Mercury: lead vocals, backing vocals, keyboards, drum machine, synth bass
Brian May: electric guitar, acoustic guitar, lead vocals, backing vocals, drum machine, synth bass, keyboards
Roger Taylor: drums, lead vocals, backing vocals, percussion, synthesiser, electric guitar, acoustic guitar
John Deacon: bass guitar, electric guitar, drum machine, synthesiser
+ David Bowie: vocals and synthesiser on 'Under Pressure'; Arif Mardin: horn arrangement on 'Staying Power'; Reinhold Mack: synth bass on 'Action This Day'; Dino Solera: saxophone on 'Action This Day'.
Recorded mid-June 1981 to mid-summer 1981 at Musicland Studios, Munich; mid-late summer 1981 at Mountain Studios, Montreux; December 1981-mid-March 1982 at Musicland Studios, Munich. Produced by Queen and Mack, Queen and David Bowie.
UK release date: 21 May 1982. US release date: 25 May 1982.
Highest chart places: UK: 4, USA: 22.

Hot Space invites you to dance. And for that reason alone, many Queen fans dismiss it. Some actively dislike it.

But Queen's difficult tenth album has aged well. In 1982, its shift of direction confused buyers, especially after the massive worldwide hits that preceded it. '*[Hot Space]* remains the sore thumb in Queen's back catalogue,' notes Dave Everley. 'But despite its reputation, this bold, flamboyant, preposterous set of songs retain[s] a peculiar charm.'

And, whilst *Hot Space* has a greater diversity of new styles than any other Queen album – the smooth reggae of 'Cool Cat'; the disco of 'Back Chat'; the rock-disco hybrids 'Dancer' and 'Put Out the Fire'; the sub-Prince pop/funk of 'Staying Power'; the '80s rhythm and blues of 'Body Language'; the '80s synth-pop of 'Action This Day' and 'Calling All Girls' – over thirty years on the album can be re-evaluated as a genuine and brave attempt at something new. Songs such as 'Dancer', 'Body Language' and 'Put Out the Fire' sound forced but much of the album is certainly worthy of the Queen name, despite the notable absence of multi-layered vocals and loud drums, and the much-reduced contribution from Brian May's guitar.

There is also one of their greatest songs: 'Under Pressure'.

Perhaps it was all a year too soon. Michael Jackson's *Thriller*, released six months later, would meld pop, post-disco, rock and funk would become the world's best-selling album with seven of its nine tracks becoming top 10 singles on the Billboard Hot 100 chart between 1982 and 1984. The band's next album, *The Works* is very much a refinement of the sounds first heard on *Hot Space*, with added commercialism and rock bluster.

Hot Space was recorded in three phases: firstly, at Musicland Studio in Munich for several weeks in the early part of summer 1981, then moving to Mountain Studios until late August or early September 1981. Queen went back on the road in September 1981 for the second half of their *The Game* tour and resumed work on *Hot Space* at Musicland in December 1981 until March 1982.

That album taught me that even if you're in a band as a guitar player, music doesn't have to be driven by guitar – it's about the song, first. But I think the main thing is that Queen actually did an album like that – it was the fans' least favourite, but it was one of my favourites because it took a risk and branched out. All those synth parts they did and horns, I could always hear them with guitar in my head somehow. But quite oddly enough, or coincidentally enough, the title Hot Space is exactly what it meant: it's all the space between the music. That's what makes it funky.

Nuno Bettencourt, *Songfacts*, May 2015

Roger Taylor is not quite so forgiving: 'I always thought that *Hot Space* was the worst album we ever did. Freddie and I thought it was going to be great and it was absolute shit. I think we got bogged down in the studio. Blame the '80s. There was a lot of awful, dreadful shit in the '80s.' [9]

'Staying Power' (Freddie Mercury)
Released as a single b-side, 9 August 1982 (UK), b/w 'Back Chat'. Released as a single a-side, November 1982 (US), b/w 'Back Chat'.

'Staying Power' is a wonderful song – sharp, sassy, fun. Freddie Mercury is 100% committed to this track. Listen to his strong vocals, his complex, syncopated keyboard arrangements, his fabulous backing vocals. Sitting somewhere between the Minneapolis funk of Prince, the LA pop of Michael Jackson and the harder New York soul-funk of Rick James, this is all-in-all a remarkable song. 'The Prophet's Song' it ain't.

'Staying Power' was performed live in 1982 and 1984. This was much faster and harder with Brian May converting the synth bass into a powerful guitar riff and John Deacon playing funky rhythm guitar. An extended version is available only on a US promo single.

'Dancer' (Brian May)

A bastard rock-disco mess. You feel that Brian May's heart isn't really in it, despite some stingingly loud guitar. The bass line was played by May on an Oberheim OB-Xa synthesiser. John Deacon does not take part.

'Back Chat' (John Deacon)

Released as a single a-side, 9 August 1982, b/w 'Staying Power'. UK: 40. Released as a single b-side, November 1982 (US), b/w 'Staying Power'. An out-of-character track, yes – disco with a hammering guitar solo – 'Back Chat' is one of those lost Queen songs that is ripe for re-evaluation. Pinned down by a four-to-the-floor processed drum pattern, Deacon's throbbing bass and Mercury's exuberant vocal, Brian May's contribution is limited to a short but magnificent guitar solo. He plays this on a Telecaster in the video, so may well have used the same instrument in the studio. 'Back Chat' was performed in a fast, tight, exciting arrangement in 1982 and a fabulous version is on *Queen on Fire – Live at the Bowl*. The use of real drums here gives the live version a boost.

About 20 seconds were removed for the single, and the song was remixed. An extended mix was released on the 'Back Chat' 12' single, 9 August 1982. Almost seven minutes in length, the 12' mix adds lots more Brian May guitar.

'The best thing about that track was the percussion solo,' says Roger Taylor, 'but then I would say that, wouldn't I?' [10]

'Body Language' (Freddie Mercury)

Released as a single a-side, 19 April 1982, b/w 'Life is Real (Song for Lennon)'. UK: 25. US: 11. Released on the UK 12' single for 'The Show Must Go On', 14 October 1991.

Dominated by a terrific coiling synth-bass line later reused for 'A Kind of Magic', 'Body Language' is hypnotic but a difficult song to like. It's effectively an empty disco rewrite of 'Get Down Make Love' with minimal input from the other members of Queen.

'Never the most restrained performer to start off with,' says Alex Petredis, 'Mercury nearly ruptures himself trying to make *Hot Space* work, with some fairly excruciating results. 'Give ME your BOD-AAAAY! SEX-AAAAAAAY SEX-AAAAY BOD-AAAAY! Look at MEEEEEEE! Look at MEEEEEE!' he cries on 'Body Language'. It comes as a relief when they finally slope off the dancefloor, defeated.' [11]

Freddie Mercury would be better able to express his love for disco and R&B (and for the gay lifestyle) in his solo work.

Performed live in 1982. There is a remix of 'Body Language' on the 1991 re-issue of *Hot Space*. This adds electronic drums, more guitar and pushes forward otherwise unheard piano. It's great.

Queen's debut album was recorded during studio downtime usually between 3am and 7am, over six months from June to December 1972. It was ridiculous, catchy and a whole lot of fun.
(Island Records)

In *Queen II* we start to hear the band's sound coalesce into three styles: the rocker, the ballad and the anthem. Side Black established Freddie Mercury as a writer and musician of rare talent.
(Island Records)

Sheer Heart Attack was Queen's commercial breakthrough and first masterpiece. Freddie Mercury broadened Queen's sound to include and baroque balladry ('Lily of the Valley', 'In the Lap of the Gods … Revisited'), music hall pastiche ('Bring Back That Leroy Brown'), arch nastiness ('Flick of the Wrist') and a superb piano-led bubble-gum-pop hit single ('Killer Queen'). Brian May added the powerful ('Brighton Rock'), the poetic ('Dear Friends') and the Queen song performed more than any another ('Now I'm Here').
(Island Records)

If you take it seriously then *A Night at the Opera* is utterly absurd — pretentious, silly overblown nonsense. If you don't, it's smart, creative, camp and a great deal of fun. Either way the album would change the lives of the four men in Queen.
(Island Records)

A Day at the Races is Queen's first self-produced album, and the second to borrow its title from a film by the Marx Brothers. *A Day at the Races* would explore many of the same musical styles and genres as *A Night at the Opera* but there are fewer new ideas than on any previous Queen album. *(Island Records)*

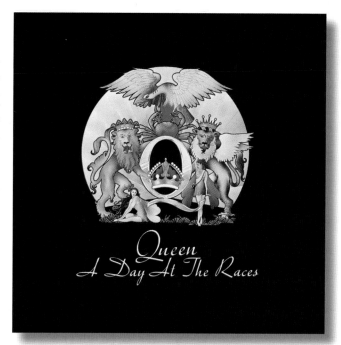

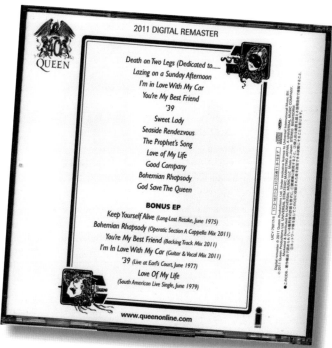

The back cover of the 2011 CD re-master of *A Night at the Opera* with bonus tracks. *(Island Records)*

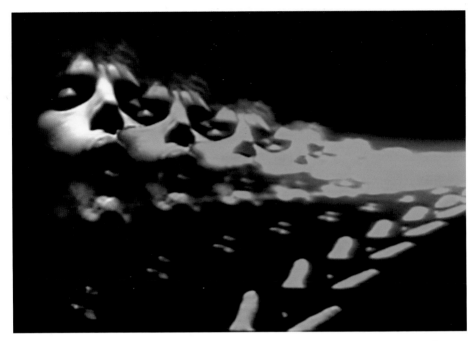

Recorded in four hours at a cost of just £4,500 and directed by Bruce Gowers at Elstree Studios, the promotional film for 'Bohemian Rhapsody' is still considered innovative today. *(EMI)*

News of the World. Queen's response, to punk and disco, if perhaps unconsciously, was to strip down their sound, hold back on the overdubs and keep the songs as simple as possible. Of course, with Queen, back-to-basics includes a cod-jazz ballad, a six-and-a-half-minute song divided into three acts, and a rumination on the death of Brian May's pet cat. *(Island Records)*

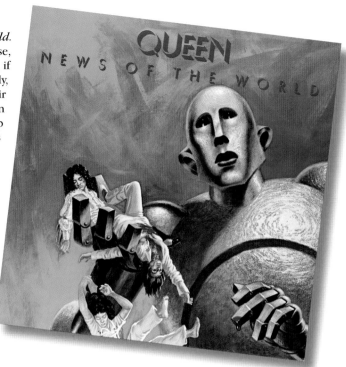

Brian May's hands turn noticeably blue. The promo for 'Spread Your Wings', January 1978. *(EMI)*

Jazz. Queen's fractured, musically-diverse seventh album was their first to be recorded outside the UK, necessitated by punitive taxation of the band's new-found massive wealth. For the first time, the songs on a Queen album are of a 'standard' length—all around three or four minutes. There are no lengthy epics or clever vignettes here. *(Island Records)*

The Game. There's an argument that suggests that Queen's first seven albums were collections of songs that worked together. All of this changed in 1979. Suddenly Queen had an eye on the singles charts. *(Island Records)*

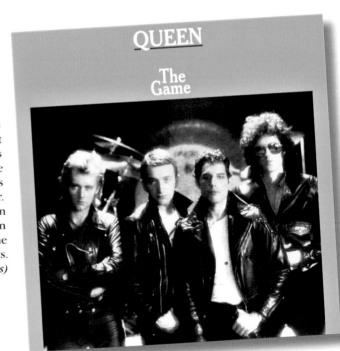

'Now, in my opinion, the soundtrack to *Flash Gordon* is a work of absolute genius. Queen did one hell of a job and it should have won them an Oscar, or at the very least a BAFTA. No doubt about it. If you don't agree with me, go and kick yourself up the bloody arse. You're wrong!' Brian Blessed *(Island Records)*

Hot Space invites you to dance. And for that reason alone, many Queen fans dismiss it. Some actively dislike it. But Queen's difficult tenth album has aged well. In 1982, its shift of direction confused buyers, especially after the massive worldwide hits that preceded it. Perhaps it was all a year too soon.
(Island Records)

Queen were always a massive live draw, with state-of-the-art lighting and a powerful, varied back catalogue. Their November 1981 performances in Montreal were recorded for posterity and released in 2007 on the CD/DVD *Queen Rock Montreal. (EMI)*

'A partial return to form that attempted to integrate the group's trademark classicism with their later affection for pop idioms, *The Works* was undoubtedly designed to please many and offend few. And therein lay the problem … there was little present to truly flabbergast the listener. This was the sound of Queen lite.'
Martin Power
(Island Records)

A Kind of Magic. Two months after the triumph of Live Aid, Queen returned to Musicland in Munich to commence the recording of their twelfth studio album. 'Like every Queen album since *Jazz*, *A Kind of Magic* was a so-so album, cleverly loaded with two or three potential hit singles.' Mark Blake *(Island Records)*

'*Live Aid*, on July 13, 1985, was the greatest live concert ever staged and a day that no one who saw it will ever forget. Apart from the audiences at the transatlantic events (72,000 at Wembley Stadium in London; 99,000 at the John F Kennedy Stadium in Philadelphia), it was estimated that another two billion people in 60 countries watched it on television. There was one thing that everybody agreed on: Queen's mind-blowing 20-minute set stole the show.' Peter Stanford, *The Telegraph*, 24 September 2011 *(Band Aid Trust)*

Freddie's iconic performance at Live Aid gave Queen a new pop audience and a reason to carry on. *(Band Aid Trust)*

The Miracle was the first album to be recorded after Freddie Mercury's diagnosis and represented a dramatic return to form after the five patchy-at-best albums since *Jazz*. At the time there was every expectation that Queen's thirteenth studio album would be their last. *(Island Records)*

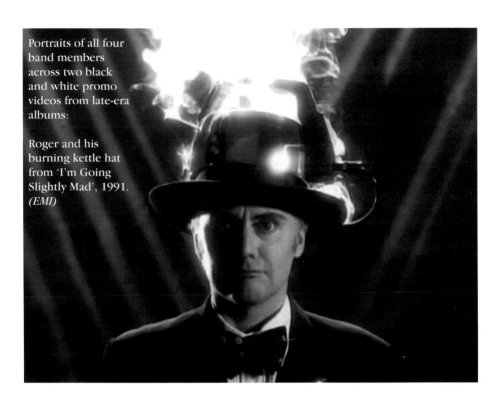

Portraits of all four band members across two black and white promo videos from late-era albums:

Roger and his burning kettle hat from 'I'm Going Slightly Mad', 1991. *(EMI)*

Freddie goes bananas, also from 'I'm Going Slightly Mad'. *(EMI)*

John and Brian from the rather more contemplative 'Those Were the Days of Our Lives' video, 1991. *(EMI)*

Sessions for *Innuendo,* Queen's ruminative and dark last studio album in Freddie's lifetime, followed hard upon those for *The Miracle.* After ten years of writing and recording singles and album filler, *Innuendo* was developed as a unified whole. The idea of the all-important hit single was pushed back. This time, the concept of a magnificent, grandiose, elegant album of great songs was paramount. *(Island Records)*

This final album, beautifully recorded and surprisingly optimistic and life-affirming in tone, stands alongside Queen's other work. The realisation that no-one is invincible after all is a key theme of the songs here. On *Made in Heaven,* finally, it seems, Queen have grown up. *(Island Records)*

The closing ceremony of the London Olympics, 12 August 2012. One of the highlights of the ceremony was Brian and Roger performing 'We Will Rock You' with British pop diva Jessie J. *(BBC)*

Freddie's blue plaque in Feltham *(Andrew Wild)*

This classical album featuring pieces by Dvorak and Smetana was released in 1962 and re-released in 1971 - could this be the source of the title of Queen's most famous song? *(Decca)*

'Action This Day' (Roger Taylor)

An attempt to inject some life into *Hot Space*, 'Action this Day' has a catchy chorus, a driving vocal from Freddie Mercury and – yes! – a saxophone solo.

'If synthesisers were available to the likes of Little Richard and Fats Domino in the Fifties, their version of rock and roll might well have sounded like 'Action this Day',' writes Martin Power. 'To everyone's relief, things didn't work out that way.' [12]

The live versions from 1982 have May's lashing guitar pushing the song from 'good' to 'almost great' Queen, but even then, something is missing – none of them sound like they really mean it.

'Put Out the Fire' (Brian May)

Released as a single b-side in the US in July 1982, b/w 'Calling All Girls'.
A not-wholly-convincing mixture of rock and pop. Everyone seems to be trying hard to inject some life into the song. Other than May's solo – exciting, ragged, brief and recorded, reportedly, while he was wasted after a night at the Sugar Shack – this is sleepwalking music.

Performed live on the final set of dates in 1982, slipped in before 'Dragon Attack' as part of the 'Now I'm Here' medley.

'Life Is Real (Song for Lennon)' (Freddie Mercury)

Released as a single b-side, 19 April 1982, b/w 'Body Language'.
This touching, lush tribute to John Lennon appropriates the descending bass runs, piano chordings and sharp drum sound from Lennon's own 'Mother' from *John Lennon / Plastic Ono Band*. As tributes go, it's very fine indeed. Quite why this was the b-side to 'Body Language' – the band's follow-up to 'Under Pressure' – and not the a-side is a question only EMI can answer.

'Because of his status,' Mercury said to *Melody Maker* in 1981, before sessions for the album had commenced, '[John Lennon] could do that kind of preaching and affect people's thoughts. But to do this you have to have a certain amount of intellect and magic together, and the John Lennons are few and far between. People with mere talent, like me, have not got the ability or power.'

Performed live a few times in August 1982.

'Calling All Girls' (Roger Taylor)

Released as a single in the US in July 1982, b/w 'Put Out the Fire'.
A bouncy, commercial shuffle – not so far from Taylor's solo album *Fun in Space*, and redolent of the prevailing pop of Duran Duran and Human League.

'Calling All Girls' is driven by Deacon's off-beat bass, a muted electric guitar and Taylor's acoustic. With its stirring chorus and bluesy lead guitar (possibly played by Roger Taylor) it sounds nothing like Queen and is a refreshing highlight of *Hot Space*.

Performed live in 1982.

'Las Palabras De Amor (The Words of Love)' (Brian May)

Released as a single a-side, 1 June 1982, b/w 'Cool Cat'. UK: 17. Released on the UK CD single for 'The Show Must Go On', 14 October 1991 and on *Greatest Hits III*, 8 November 1999.

Brian May's best song on this album is a power ballad and a close cousin to the anthemic Queen sound of the 1970s. Swirling keyboards, layers of acoustic guitar, genuine drums, massed backing vocals, double-tracked Freddie: this song works hard to be the antithesis of 'Body Language'. But in the context of the hard funk elsewhere on *Hot Space*, it's decidedly flaccid.

'Las Palabras De Amor (The Words of Love)' is known to have been performed only once in the classic Queen period – by Brian May as a teasing intro to 'Love of My Life' at Milton Keynes on 5 June 1982. The full song was performed a handful of times, sung by Brian May and with the rest of the band accompanying, on South American Q+PR dates in 2008 and 2015.

'Cool Cat' (Freddie Mercury and John Deacon)

Released as a single b-side, 1 June 1982, b/w 'Las Palabras De Amor (The Words of Love)'.

'Cool Cat' has a very laid-back reggae feel. It was written and entirely performed by Mercury and Deacon: the clean, bright electric rhythm guitar sound and popping bass come straight from the Chic songbook. Freddie sings the song in falsetto, at times going right to the top of his range. The song was mostly finished when Deacon and Mercury played it for David Bowie at Mountain Studios in summer 1981: Bowie added backing vocals but later requested for these to be removed, delaying the release of the album.

'Under Pressure' (Queen / Bowie)

Released as a single a-side, 26 October 1981, b/w 'Soul Brother'. UK: 1. US: 29.

The first 'Queen +' collaboration, infectious and durable, remains the best. Very few people could give Freddie Mercury a run for his money in both charisma and vocal chops. David Bowie heads that list, giving us not only one of the best Queen songs, but one of the best by anyone, period. The extended four-part bridge (2:04 to 3:31) also pushes 'Under Pressure' into unknown territory for major hit singles.

'[Bowie] was just around,' Freddie Mercury told Rudi Dolezal in 1984, 'We were recording in the studio and he just said 'oh, maybe I'll come in and just see what happens'. So, it wasn't planned. If it's planned, then it's boring. We were just fooling around to see what happens, and suddenly this song started taking shape and we said, 'oh that's quite nice, let's work on it a bit' and the result of that was 'Under Pressure'.'

Mark Blake writes in *Is This the Real Life?*: 'Bowie insisted that he and Mercury shouldn't hear what the other had sung, swapping verses blind, which helped give the song its cut-and-paste feel.'

'It was evolved in an unusual way,' explains Brian May. 'We [all] worked on the backing track together, and once we had a backing track that we liked, David's idea was to get everyone to go into the vocal booth and sing the first thing that came into their heads. We'd then compile [these ideas] and see if it suggested a way the song should go. Some of Freddie's takes survived to the final vocal. It was David who decided what the song should actually be about. The song does sound a jigsaw puzzle, but I think it works amazingly well.' [13]

Contemporary interviews suggest that the lyrics were mostly by Bowie. It seems certain that Bowie wrote the very 'unQueen' line 'it's the terror of knowing what this world is about, watching some good friends screaming 'Let me out''.

The music must be a team effort between Queen and Bowie as 'Under Pressure' started as a rough, tough but unfinished Roger Taylor-written demo called 'Feel Like' (or perhaps 'Let's Make It Right'). Many of the elements are there – Brian May's restrained arpeggio guitar work, Taylor's clockwork drumming and some of the vocal melodies. But that iconic two-note bass line is missing. [14]

As is, of course, the song's other big star: Bowie himself.

There's no doubt that the very presence of Bowie galvanised Queen to write a song that is simultaneously simple in execution but complex in structure. The arrangement, whilst free from the Queen-trademark block guitar and vocal harmonies, is sublime.

0:00 A sharp stopped hi-hat opens the song, with finger snaps, echoing claps and *that* bass line. Piano joins at 0:03, guitar arpeggios are added at 0:12 (a recurring element of Roger Taylor's songs) with a synth motif below, possibly played by David Bowie. At 0:20 the guitar arpeggio is double-tracked and Mercury's scat singing is added.

0:20 The first verse grows from the intro sequence with the word 'pressure'. The sound thickens with piano, bass and synthesiser. Vocals are shared by Mercury and Bowie. The first phrase ('pressure') is Bowie, double-tracked. The second phrase starts with a harmony between them ('pushing down on me') then Bowie double-tracked ('pressing down on you no man asks for'), both together ('under pressure'), then Mercury alone ('that brings a building down, splits a family in two') and Bowie double-tracked ('puts people on streets'). Some classic Mercury scatting and interjections ('that's OK!') take the song to the bridge. We aren't yet one minute into the song and already the invention is rife.

0:55 The snare drum tempo doubles for Bowie's 'It's the terror of knowing what the world is about', joined by a Mercury harmony for 'let me out'. The two-note synthesiser motif from the introduction reappears here. Mercury takes the lead for the soaring 'pray tomorrow gets me higher', and Bowie's remarkable staccato vocal for 'pressure on people, people on streets' uses a distinctive choppy rhythm directly against Taylor's cymbal accents.

1:11   A brief return to the bass/piano motifs of the introduction.

1:20   The second verse is sung mostly by Mercury in thrilling free-phrased falsetto ('chippin' around, kick my brains around the floor / these are the days it never rains but it pours'). Bowie adds ethereal step-wise ascending backing vocals. Mercury sings the rest of this section with scat-lyrics, building the tension.

1:45   The release of the reprise of the 'terror of knowing section'. Freddie's closing, climbing phrase ('tomorrow makes me high, high, high') resembles to a similar figure in 'Don't Stop Me Now' ('I feel ali-hi-hi-hive!').

2:04   The first part of the remarkable closing section. Bowie and Mercury quietly sing 'turned away from it all like a blind man', Bowie in low register, Mercury in falsetto. They are accompanied by organ chords and taps on the hi-hat. The line 'keep coming up with love but it's so slashed and torn' must be Bowie's work.

2:18   A guitar figure (May has been almost silent since the introduction) leads into a rising crescendo as the arrangement gets louder. Taylor's drumming is more and more intense, Bowie sings 'love, love, love' as Freddie's amazing falsetto singing, full of tension and surely his best in any Queen song, takes us to a phenomenal climax as Bowie sings 'Insanity laughs under pressure we're breaking' as the pressure does indeed break as we finally revert to the home key. The thirty-two seconds of 'Under Pressure' from 2:04 to 2:36 rank as career highlights of not only Queen and Bowie, but of much of rock music. Listen to Pink Floyd's 'Echoes' (17:20 to 19:12) for a similar build and release.

2:36   The resolution of 'why can't we give ourselves one more chance?' with the last phrase echoing Mercury's 'give love' into fade out as descending bass guitar lifts the song to another climax with Bowie's "cause love's such an old-fashioned word, and love dares you to care for the people on the edge of the night ... this is our last dance, this is ourselves'. The lead melody of this rising phrase is the same as the backing vocals in the second chorus. This whole section – music and lyrics – does not appear in the original demo. It's very clever, and probably Bowie's work, yet very Queenesque in the way a repeating motif gives a cohesion to the song.

3:31   The final section reprises the bass guitar, piano, synthesiser and finger snaps from the introduction, ending on an unresolved piano phase and fade out.

'Under Pressure' was performed live in every Queen concert in 1981, 1984, 1985 and 1986. Freddie would sing Bowie's parts with Roger Taylor providing strong vocal backup. David Bowie performed the song with Queen and Annie Lennox at the Freddie Mercury tribute show in 1992 and added the song to his own set-list in 1995 (as the closing number of the main set), 1996, 1997, 2000 (again, as the set closer), 2003 and 2004. For these shows Gail Ann Dorsey would impressively cover both Freddie's vocal and John Deacon's bass lines. It was revived on tours with Adam Lambert.

An edited version is on *Greatest Hits II*, October 1991. One repeat of 'this is our last dance' is removed. A remix on *Classic Queen*, 1992 is a very clean-sounding mix with some variants in the vocal tracks. A new mix, the 'Under Pressure (rah mix)' was released on *Greatest Hits III* in 1999 and as a single (UK: 14). This new mix combines existing, unused and new elements to create an unnecessary version of 'Under Pressure'. There is a variant of the rah mix called 'Under Pressure (Club 2000 mix)', also released in 1999. The 'Under Pressure (Mike Spencer mix)', 1999 is another very clean mix, this time by Mike Spencer, a British producer who has worked with Kylie Minogue, Jamiroquai, Rudimental and Ellie Goulding.

Alexis Petridis: "Under Pressure' [is] the kind of ludicrous, brilliant, lyrically baffling song that no other band would have thought of recording.' [15]

'There are so many hooks packed in to 'Under Pressure',' writes Robert Ham, 'but none better than that simple, infectious bass line. If hearing it doesn't send an electric charge up your spine, you might be dead inside.' [16]

Other contemporary songs
'Soul Brother'
Released as a single b-side, 26 October 1981, b/w 'Under Pressure', in the US as the b-side to 'Heaven for Everyone' (Autumn 1996) and on the 2011 re-release of *Hot Space*. It's a jokey song, written by Freddie Mercury with lyrics made up of references to previous Queen songs – 'He's my best friend he's my champion / And he will rock you / 'Cause he's the saviour of the universe / He can make you keep yourself alive'.

'Sex Show'
Recorded during sessions for *Hot Space* – it might be part of another song.

'There Must Be More to Life Than This'
On which producer *du jour* William Orbit resurrects an unused Queen original from 1981 – later re-recorded by Queen for *The Works* (but unreleased) and by Freddie Mercury (very Queen in sound and execution) for *Mr Bad Guy* – and adds the vocals from an unfinished version by Michael Jackson.

'Basically, it's a love and peace song,' Freddie Mercury told David Wigg in 1985. 'I really don't like to write message songs but this the way this one just came out. It's all to do with 'why do people get themselves with so many problems?' It's just one of those songs that I had for a while ... nearly two years ago and Michael happened to hear it and he liked it and if it worked out we would have done it together, but now it's 1985, it's my solo project and I wanted it on there so I did it without his help. He's going to cry'.

So, we have the odd creation of a fake duet between dead superstars who sound like they are singing in a bathroom along the corridor. Get outta town. And, May, leave that guitar with me. Released on *Queen Forever* in 2014.

The Works (1984)

Personnel:
Freddie Mercury: lead vocals, backing vocals, keyboards, sampler
Brian May: electric guitar, acoustic guitar, backing vocals
Roger Taylor: electronic and acoustic drums, backing vocals, vocoder, sampler, percussion, drum machine, synthesiser
John Deacon: bass guitar, acoustic guitar
+ Fred Mandel – synthesisers on 'Radio Gaga', 'Tear it Up', 'Man on the Prowl', 'I Want to Break Free' and 'Hammer to Fall', piano on 'Radio Gaga'.
Recorded between August 1983 and October-November 1983, Record Plant Studios, Los Angeles; January 1984 at Musicland Studios, Munich. Produced by Queen and Mack.
UK release date: 27 February 1984. US release date: 28 February 1984.
Highest chart places: UK: 2, USA: 23.

Following the relative failure of *Hot Space*, Queen's eleventh album is a partial return to the commercial sound of *The Game*, but with a contemporary sheen. Significantly, *The Works* was recorded at the Record Plant in Los Angeles, favoured by slick American rock acts such as Boston (debut album, 1976), Fleetwood Mac (*Rumours* and *Mirage*, 1976 and 1982), Cheap Trick (*Heaven Tonight* and *Dream Police*, 1978-1979), Blue Öyster Cult (*Mirrors*, 1979) and Kiss (*Killers*, 1982). Brian May had recorded his *Starfleet Project* at the Record Plant in April 1983. These were Queen's first sessions outside Europe, except for horn overdubs on *Hot Space* which they did not attend.

'A partial return to form that attempted to integrate the group's trademark classicism with their later affection for pop idioms,' notes Martin Power, '*The Works* was undoubtedly designed to please many and offend few. And therein lay the problem ... there was little present to truly flabbergast the listener. This was the sound of Queen lite.' [17]

'Radio Ga Ga', the lead-off single released a month ahead of the album, was their first top ten hit for three years. Queen, at last, were back.

According to Adam Under and Patrick Lemieux in *The Queen Chronology*, a display at the Stormtroopers in Stilettos exhibition in London, February-March 2011 included early artwork of a cassette inlay for *The Works*. The track-listing on this cassette is 'Tear It Up', 'Whipping Boy', 'I Want to Break Free', 'Machines (or 'Back to Humans')', 'Man On Fire', 'Take Another Little Piece Of My Heart', 'It's A Hard Life', 'Your Heart Again', 'Man On The Prowl', 'Radio Ga Ga' (listed as 'Radio Caca'), 'Hammer to Fall', 'Keep Passing the Open Windows' and 'Man Made Paradise'. Many of the exhibits are now housed at a permanent exhibition in Montreux.

'Radio Ga Ga' (Roger Taylor)

Released as a single a-side, 23 January 1984, b/w 'I Go Crazy'. UK: 2. US: 16.
'Radio Ga Ga' takes the pop sensibilities of *The Game*, the modern sounds
of *Hot Space*, and the power of a Queen concert to create a massive, catchy,
hugely important worldwide hit. The influence of Herbie Hancock's 'Rockit',
a UK hit in summer 1983, is very evident. Roger Taylor presumably wrote
'Radio Ga Ga' on the keyboards, rather than the guitar as previously – this
development led to Taylor writing several important songs for the band in the
coming years: 'A Kind of Magic', 'The Invisible Man', 'These Are the Days of Our
Lives' and 'Heaven for Everyone'. Brian May's contribution is limited to a slide
guitar solo on his Red Special.

'Roger and I started on this together, chucking some ideas around,' says
Brian May. 'We split in the end and Roger's half become 'Radio Ga Ga' and my
half became 'Machines'.' [18]

The influence of the promotional video for 'Radio Ga Ga' should not be
underestimated. Previous Queen videos had been, for the most part, straight
forward performances, usually on stage or in a studio. Or in Roger Taylor's
back garden. Only 'Save Me', with its animated doves, 'Body Language', semi-
naked goings-on in a communal shower, and 'Calling All Girls' – just watch it
and giggle – bucked that trend. By 1984, music videos had gone mainstream
and during the 1980s music videos became *de rigueur* for recording artists.
Directors and musicians began to explore and expand the form and style of
promotional videos, often adding a storyline or plot to the music video. 'Radio
Ga Ga' includes excerpts from the 1927 film *Metropolis* and includes the key
scene where the fully costumed band encourage a large white-clad crowd to
clap along in time. From 1984, this became a key element of every Queen
concert: the song was performed live in 1984, 1985 and 1986, usually as the
last song of the main set, or as the first encore. It was also performed both with
Paul Rodgers and Adam Lambert.

The 12" mix, released in January 1984, extends the song to seven minutes
with repeated instrumental passages. 'Radio Ga Ga' was included on *Greatest
Hits II* in 1991, edited with an early fade-out.

'Tear It Up' (Brian May)

Released as a single b-side, 10 September 1984, b/w 'Hammer to Fall'.
A by-the-book Brian May rocker, with the heavily-gated drum sound of the mid-
1980s. The riff was based on May's extemporised performances within 'Fat
Bottomed Girls' on the *Hot Space* tour.

'Tear It Up' was performed live, 1984-1986. During 1984 and 1985, it opened
the set after the band came on stage to an excerpt from 'Machines (Or 'Back to
Humans')'; in 1986 it usually followed 3 or 4 older songs at the top of the set.

'It's a Hard Life' (Freddie Mercury)

Released as a single a-side, 16 July 1984, b/w 'Is This the World We Created...?'.

UK: 6. US: 72. Also on *Greatest Hits II*, 1991.
The welcome return of piano, harmonic guitars and backing vocals gives this a classic Queen sound. The mostly instrumental version from *Greatest Karaoke Hits* shows off the backing track to great effect; this could have been recorded in 1977-1978.

The beginning of the song is based on Pagliacci's aria 'Vesti la Giubba': the lyrics 'Ridi, Pagliaccio, sul tuo amore infranto!' ('Laugh, clown, for your love is broken') were replaced in 'It's a Hard Life' with the phrase 'I don't want my freedom, there's no reason for living with a broken heart'.

The opening piano chords give a neat twist on the ballad section of 'Bohemian Rhapsody'. Whilst not particularly inventive the song is packed with melody and has a short, catchy guitar solo. 'It's a Hard Life' was brilliantly performed on *The Works* tour in 1985-1986. It was also part of the 2010 Prince's Trust Concert when it was sung, exceedingly well, by *Mister* Tom Chaplin of Keane. [19]

An extended mix was created for the 12" single. This adds an extra chorus, vocal breakdown and reprise of the guitar solo into the central section.

'Man on the Prowl' (Freddie Mercury)
Released as a single b-side, 26 November 1984, b/w 'Thank God It's Christmas'. Another Mercury rock-and-roll pastiche, retreading 'Crazy Little Thing Called Love', but without the same *joie de vivre*. The rollicking piano is by the Canadian session musician Fred Mandel, who had toured with Queen in 1982 and contributed to 'Radio Ga Ga', 'Hammer to Fall' and 'I Want to Break Free' as well as solo albums by Brian May and Freddie Mercury.

'Man on the Prowl' was originally slated as the fifth single from *The Works* before being replaced with (and placed on the b-side of) 'Thank God It's Christmas'. The extended 12" is twice as long as it needs to be.

'Machines (Or 'Back to Humans')' (Brian May / Roger Taylor)
Released as a single b-side, 2 April 1984, b/w 'I Want to Break Free'.
A furiously experimental track, with bubbling Fairlight, synthesised drums, grunting guitar, counterpoint bass, processed vocals and a great lead vocal from Freddie. It's mostly on a single chord and has no verses to speak of. It's an unqualified success. Casual Queen fans probably hate it.

Brian May mixed a dull instrumental version with additional guitar and excerpts from 'Ogre Battle', 'Goin' Back', 'Bohemian Rhapsody' and 'Flash's Theme' – released as the US b-side to 'I Want to Break Free'.

'I Want to Break Free' (John Deacon)
Single edit released as a single a-side (UK), 2 April 1984, b/w 'Machines (Or 'Back to Humans')', and on the 2011 re-release of *The Works*. UK: 3. Released as a single a-side (US), 2 April 1984, b/w 'Machines (Or 'Back to Humans')' [instrumental mix]. US: 45.
Deacon's double-tracked acoustic over clean electric guitar strumming of the

most basic of 12-bar blues changes (in E, guitar players, but don't be tempted to shuffle) underpins a very commercial song that was a worldwide hit in the spring of 1984.

The central solo is skilfully performed by Fred Mandel on synthesiser. The pitch bends and whammy bar glissando ape Brian May's style. You can hear May's favourite tremolo-dive for real on 'Brighton Rock' (3:14), 'Stone Cold Crazy' (1.43), 'Lost Opportunity' (3:45) and 'Headlong' (4:28).

The song's message of freedom – personal, political, sexual, spiritual, whatever – resonated with audiences all over the world. The hilarious video was banned by MTV in the US and the song stalled at 45 in the Billboard listings.

'I Want to Break Free' was performed live in 1984-1986 and both with Paul Rodgers and Adam Lambert. In these live versions the synthesiser solo in the original recording was replaced by a Brian May guitar solo.

John Deacon mixed the single version which is over a minute longer than the album version, featuring a longer introduction and an extra instrumental verse. A 7-minute remix of this is on the 12" single and on the 1991 re-release of *The Works*. This has an even longer instrumental opening with repeated instrumental verses throughout. It ends with a collage of snippets from the other songs on *The Works* – 'Radio Ga Ga', 'It's a Hard Life', 'Man on the Prowl', 'Machines (or 'Back to Humans')', 'Keep Passing the Open Windows', 'Hammer to Fall', 'Tear It Up' and 'Is This the World We Created ... ?'.

'Keep Passing the Open Windows' (Freddie Mercury)

Released as a single b-side, 26 November 1984, b/w 'Thank God It's Christmas'. Originally written for the film version of John Irving's 1981 book *Hotel New Hampshire*. 'Keep Passing the Open Windows' is a recurrent phrase in the film, which premiered about three weeks after the release of *The Works*. It's a straightforward, cleanly-produced Freddie Mercury pop song, with tinkling piano octaves, thrumming bass (later reused for 'A Kind of Magic') and loud guitar with occasional changes in dynamics. Harmless if not particularly memorable, 'Keep Passing the Open Windows' is unlikely to be listed amongst anyone's favourite Queen songs, despite the skill in execution.

The extended 12" version has around an additional two minutes of burbling synthesisers on a single chord.

'Hammer to Fall' (Brian May)

Released as a single a-side, 10 September 1984, b/w 'Tear It Up'. UK: 13. Also on *Greatest Hits II*, 1991.

A rather basic rocker, of which Brian May must be very proud as it's been a mainstay of every Queen, solo and Queen+ tour since 1984, including the band's appearance at Live Aid. There's no denying the power in Freddie Mercury's vocal performance: effortless and controlled, but loud and virile.

Performed live 1984-1986 (with Spike Edney on second guitar), and with Paul Rodgers and Adam Lambert.

The Headbanger's Mix was released on 12" single. This is an extended remix with a new guitar/drums opening and additional guitar solos very reminiscent of 'Now I'm Here'. This is more easily available on the 2011 re-release of *The Works*. An edit of this mix was released as a single a-side, removing the intro and most of the guitar solos. Released as an instrumental as part of *The eYe*.

'Is This the World We Created... ?' (Freddie Mercury / Brian May)
Released as a single b-side, 16 July 1984, b/w 'It's a Hard Life'.

The last song written and recorded for *The Works* is a rare writing collaboration between Mercury and May – only 'Bijou' and 'Mother Love' also share this joint writing credit. It's a touching ballad, with May's acoustic guitar providing the only accompaniment to Mercury's reverb-laden lead vocal.

Whereas May's lyrics would often resort to cliché and pathos, Mercury's here are more direct: 'You know that everyday a helpless child is born / Who needs some loving care inside a happy home / Somewhere a wealthy man is sitting on his throne / Waiting for life to go by / If there's a God in the sky looking down / What can he think of what we've done / To the world that he created?'

'Is This the World We've Created?' is an antidote to the typical Queen bombast – it sits alongside 'Dear Friends', 'Lily of the Valley', 'Love of My Life', '39', 'My Melancholy Blues' and 'You Take My Breath Away' as a quiet song that demonstrates Queen's depth and breadth in song writing and performance.

The original mix of this track is rumoured to have Freddie on piano in additional to May's guitar. If so, it's never been heard. Generations of wannabe Brians have been frustrated when trying to play along to 'Is This the World We Created...?' as his guitar is tuned down half a step, presumably to more comfortably fit Mercury's vocal range.

The song was performed live in 1984-1986, including, memorably, as part of the finale to the London Live Aid concert in 1985.

Other contemporary songs
'I Go Crazy'
Released as a single b-side, 23 January 1984, b/w 'Radio Ga Ga', and on the 1991 and 2011 re-releases of *The Works*.

This track originates from the *Hot Space* sessions and an unreleased Queen + David Bowie collaboration called 'I Don't Want to be a Rolling Stone'.

'Whipping Boy'
'Whipping Boy', from the original running order for *The Works*, is probably an alternative title for 'I Go Crazy'.

'Thank God It's Christmas'
Written by Brian May and Roger Taylor. Released as a single a-side, 26

November 1984, b/w 'Man on the Prowl' and 'Keep Passing Open Windows'. UK: 21. Also released on *Greatest Hits III*, 1999, and on the 2011 re-release of *The Works*. A pointless Christmas single.

'I Dream of Christmas'
Written by Brian May as a contender for Queen's 1984 year-end single but dropped in favour of 'Thank God It's Christmas'. The song would later be donated to Anita Dobson. Brian produced, played guitar and sang backing vocals on this 1987 version, and John Deacon can be heard on bass.

'I Feel Like a Man on Fire'
'I Feel Like a Man on Fire' is a Roger Taylor track, released on his album *Strange Frontier* (as 'Man on Fire') in June 1984 and included in the original running order for *The Works*.

'Take Another Little Piece of My Heart'
'Take Another Little Piece of My Heart' is the original title for 'Let Me Live', completed in 1995 for *Made in Heaven*.

'Let Me in Your Heart Again'
'Let Me in Your Heart Again' was released on Queen Forever in 2014. It features a full-tilt Freddie vocal with a classic late 70s Queen sound, including piano, and can be readily compared to stadium anthems such as 'Somebody to Love' and 'Save Me'. Perhaps its obvious similarities to 'Hammer to Fall' prevented its completion in 1983. The song also bears a striking resemblance to 'It's Late' – both drop through their respective scales in the hook of the chorus (try singing the phrase 'let me in your heart again' over the changes to 'it's late, it's late, it's late'). The original recording was beefed up with new guitars, drums and backing vocals in 2014 and is a worthy addition to the Queen catalogue. Queen train spotters can seek out the 1987 version by Brian May's future wife, Anita Dobson. The Queen sound is certainly evident, especially in Brian May's solo.

'Let Me in Your Heart Again' is also available in a 'William Orbit mix'. This is much closer in sound and feel to the songs on *The Works*. The roaring guitars and drums have been replaced with burbling sequencers, giving the song an '80s feel, not so far away from synth-heavy pop anthems such as 'A Kind of Magic', 'One Vision' and 'Radio Ga Ga'. This might have been a huge hit in 1984. Released as a single, 3 November 2014. UK: 102

'Man-Made Paradise'
'Man-Made Paradise' was recorded by Freddie Mercury for *Mr Bad Guy* – a highlight of that underrated album. It includes some very Queen-like guitar from German session player Paul Vincent, including some harmonics, hammers-on and rising scale patterns straight from the *Play Like Brian May*

handbook. One wonders why May himself wasn't invited to take part. A demo was recorded by Mercury (or perhaps by the full band) in 1983-1984. A fragment can be heard on the documentary *Freddie Mercury – The Untold Story* (2000).

'Victory', 'State of Shock'

Michael Jackson songs, from early 1983 worked on by Jackson with Freddie Mercury. In a contemporary interview, Mercury suggests that Jackson merely used the title 'Victory' for his next album title – there is a rumoured full band Queen version of the original song from 1983-1984. If so, aural evidence is not available. 'State of Shock', meanwhile was planned as a Mercury/Jackson duet – in the end it was Mick Jagger who appeared on the final version.

'Love Kills (The Ballad)'

A song begun during sessions for The Works, and then released as Freddie Mercury's first solo single in 1984, on the same day as 'Hammer to Fall'. Only Freddie's playful vocals and layered backing vocals mark out 'Love Kills' as a Queen-related track – the backing is bubbling high-energy electro-disco courtesy of Italian producer Georgio Moroder.

Reworked for *Queen Forever* in 2014, the Queen version takes an alternative, slower very strong vocal take and adds layered guitars with a modern rock ballad production. It sounds a lot like Queen. This ballad version was performed with Adam Lambert on most of the 2014 tour of North America – it's perhaps Lambert's best work with Queen.

Footnotes

[1] Radio.com, November 2014.
[2] *Popcorn*, June 1981.
[3] Lambert also performed 'Dragon Attack' in his solo shows in 2013.
[4] *Queen Unseen*, 2015.
[5] *Freddie Mercury: This is the Real Life*, 1993.
[6] response to fan query, April 2003, published at brianmay.com.
[7] Radio.com, November 2014.
[8] *As It Began* (1992) says that Anvil Studios in London was used as well. Or perhaps this is a mistake – this same book suggests that a guitar has five strings and that the chief of Electra records is Jack Holsten.
[9] *Q magazine*, 2005.
[10] commentary on *Greatest Video Hits II*, 2003.
[11] *The Guardian*, 15 December 2011.
[12] *The Complete Guide to the Music of Queen*, 2006
[13] commentary on *Absolute Greatest*, 2009.
[14] Play a D on the 12th fret, then an A on the 12th fret. It's that simple. John Deacon, ever modest, credited the bass line to Bowie. Peter Hince: 'John thinks it's one of the best things they ever did. And Roger wished they could have done more with Bowie.'

[15] *The Guardian*, 15 December 2011.
[16] Radio.com, November 2014.
[17] *The Complete Guide to the Music of Queen*, 2006.
[18] commentary on *Absolute Greatest*, 2009.
[19] Keane sometimes performed a faithful version 'Under Pressure' between 2007 and 2014, most often as a crowd-pleasing final number at festivals. So did the Foo Fighters in 2017-2018.

One Glorious Day – Live Aid

18.41, 13 July 1985.

72,000 people at Wembley Stadium in London; 99,000 at the John F Kennedy Stadium in Philadelphia; another two *billion* people in 60 countries watching on TV.

Live Aid was a big deal.

And yet, Queen had to be pushed hard to take part. They had played to an estimated 700,000 people over two nights in Rio de Janiero earlier that year: a victory lap that would give them pause as they determined their next move. Or whether there would be a next move at all.

Organiser Bob Geldof recalled, in his autobiography: 'I traced Jim [Beach, Queen manager] all the way down to ... some little seaside resort that he was staying at, and I said, "Look, for Christ's sake, you know, what's wrong with them?" Jim said, "Oh, you know, Freddie's very sensitive." So I said, "Tell the old faggot it's gonna be the biggest thing that ever happened – this huge mega thing." So eventually they got back and said OK, they would definitely be doing it. It was the perfect stage for Freddie. He could ponce about in front of the whole world.'

Live Aid would provide the ideal answer to the 'what next?' question hanging over Queen.

'Everyone will be trying to outdo each other, which will cause a bit of friction,' said Mercury at the time. 'It makes me personally proud to be a part of it.' [1]

The London concert was opened by reliable rockers Status Quo, followed by many of the pop acts *du jour*: The Style Council, Ultravox, Spandau Ballet, Nik Kershaw, Howard Jones, Sade, and Paul Young. Phil Collins and Sting, older but only a few years into their solo careers and with a touch more credibility than many of the others on the bill, did themselves no harm by singing together on 'Every Breath You Take'. Bob Geldof's fading Boomtown Rats gave a performance of emotional resonance, despite a failed microphone. Bryan Ferry's set was so low-key as to be almost forgettable, despite the attendance of Pink Floyd's David Gilmour. Dire Straits, then mid-way through a 12-night run at the nearby Wembley Arena, performed 'Money for Nothing', soon to be an American number one. U2's twelve-minute version of 'Bad' was a career-making moment that returned all their albums to the UK charts, established them in the US, and transformed them into worldwide stars. Only the biggest UK pop royalty would follow Queen onto the London stage: David Bowie, Elton John, The Who, Paul McCartney.

With such a line-up, Queen relished the chance to pitch themselves against other acts and spent several days rehearsing their set at the Shaw Theatre in Camden, London. Queen had achieved four top twenty hits over the previous year and a half. Seven of their albums were in the UK album chart in autumn 1984. Their most recent 48-date tour, taking in the UK, Belgium, Ireland, Germany, Italy, France, the Netherlands, Austria, Brazil, New Zealand, Australia,

Japan, and, controversially, Sun City in South Africa, had finished in in mid-May. They were road-tested and ready to prove themselves.

Using the same sets, lights, backdrops and sound system as all the other artists, the focus was entirely on the songs and the performances. 'I'm not sure what we were expecting – after all, how exciting could Queen really be?' writes Dylan Jones. 'Having never been a huge fan, and never really understanding what all the fuss was about, I certainly didn't think that this was going to be the greatest stadium performance of all time.' [2]

From the moment he came on stage, dressed in a tight white singlet so that those two billion people could pick him out, Freddie Mercury was effervescent, hyped up, and ready to entertain. Freddie places himself at the piano stage right – a knowing half-grin on his face – runs though some octaves to test sound levels and counts out the ballad section of 'Bohemian Rhapsody'. The crowd at Wembley sing along from the first line.

The whole audience knew the song and, after the initial roar or recognition, sang along. The crowd ... were at the point of needing a lift. Queen gave it to them and were magnificent.
Peter 'Ratty' Hince, Freddie's roadie, *Queen Unseen*, 2015

The BBC cameraman is close enough for TV viewers to count the beads of sweat on Mercury's forehead. The first two minutes focus exclusively on Freddie Mercury. The power and control in his voice is dazzling. May's power chord ends the truncated 'Bohemian Rhapsody', and Freddie takes centre stage with his trademark mike stand as the burbling introduction to 'Radio Ga Ga' kicks in. Freddie struts, dances, nods, smiles. Here is a man in his natural element. None of it seems contrived: Freddie Mercury's charisma is palpable. The sight of Mercury, cocksure, legs apart, fist raised, encouraging the London crowd to clap to the chorus of 'Radio Ga Ga' is surely one of the defining images of the 1980s.

I remember thinking 'oh great, they've picked it up' and then I thought 'this is not a Queen audience'. This is a general audience who've bought tickets before they even knew we were on the bill. And they all did it. How did they know? Nobody told them to do it.
Brian May, quoted in *Mojo* magazine, 1999

A small skip at the end of this song shows just how keyed up Mercury was. 'Eh-oh', he sings. 'Eh-oh' sing back 72,000 voices. Six minutes into the greatest performance of his life, Mercury has the world in the palm of his hand.

From here on, the group appears invincible. Mercury teases the audience, flexing his vocal chords with some call-and-response banter before launching into 'Hammer to Fall'. A modest hit, its comic-book heavy

metal is still made for stadiums such as these. A visibly more relaxed
Brian May whips out the riff while Mercury joshes with the on-stage
cameraman, mugging into his lens, before prancing around the guitarist
like a matador goading a bull. Then, while May scrubs away, Mercury
fixes the crowd with a mischievous smile and starts tugging the end of the
microphone, now pointing out at crotch level. Less lusty rock star, more
naughty schoolboy, the twinkle in Freddie's eye suggests that he takes
none of this, including himself, seriously.
Mark Blake, *Is This the Real Life?*, 2010

'Hammer to Fall' ends with Mercury pointing his arse at 72,000 people. A
strutting 'Crazy Little Thing Called Love' – in which Brian May manages to use
three different guitars in three minutes – is 'dedicated to you all you beautiful
people tonight'. A pounding, abbreviated 'We Will Rock You' and the inevitable
'We Are the Champions', with the Wembley crowd swaying like a living
organism, close the set.

A theatrical bow, 'thank you, goodnight, we love you!'

[Freddie Mercury's] performance that day will be remembered as long
as pop is remembered … as mesmerising and as important as any by
Elvis Presley, and … as impressive as any there has ever been seen on the
Wembley stage.
Dylan Jones, *The Eighties – One Day, One Decade*, 2013

'Queen were absolutely the best band of the day,' said Bob Geldof later.
'Whatever your personal taste was irrelevant. When the day came, they played
the best, they had the best sound, they used their time to the full. They
understood the idea exactly – that it was a global jukebox. They just went and
smashed out one hit after the other. It was just unbelievable.'

Dylan Jones: 'Something in Queen's performance had crystallised not only
the afternoon, but also the very idea of Live Aid itself. There was a heaving mass
of humanity out here, genuflecting for the greater good. This was not just the
pinch point of the afternoon, not just the pinch point of Live Aid, but in some
ways the pinch point of the decade.'

Mercury and May would return later in the evening to perform a feedback-
laden version of 'Is This the World We Created…?' – a more apt song than
'Let It Be', one would argue. Viewer fatigue had already set in. McCartney's
microphone failed, Band Aid's stage-scrum version of 'Do They Know It's
Christmas' was a train wreck. Live Aid would continue for another five hours.

But the day belonged to Queen. It had been twelve years, to the day, since the
release of *Queen*. Live Aid gave them a new pop audience and a reason to carry on.

Of all Queen's 704 live performances fronted by Freddie, it remains
their most iconic, their finest hour. Live Aid gave the band the perfect

opportunity to demonstrate that, stripped of props and trappings, of their own lighting rig and sound equipment, of fog and smoke and other special effects, without even the natural magic of dusk and with fewer than twenty minutes in which to prove themselves, they were unchallenged sovereigns who still had what it took to rock the world. They would now embrace the unequivocal fact that Queen were greater than the sum of their parts.

Lesley Ann-Jones, *Freddie Mercury – The Definitive Biography*, 2012

Footnotes
[1] Interview with Simon Bates, BBC Radio 1, June 1985.
[2] *The Eighties – One Day, One Decade*, 2013.

1985–1995: In the Lap of the Gods

Live Aid catapulted Queen into the higher echelons of pop stardom. Thirteen hit singles over the next five years and a final tour in 1986 kept the band in the public eye. The UK leg of the *Magic Tour* was, at the time, the largest grossing tour in the history of British popular music.

Freddie Mercury was diagnosed with AIDS in April 1987. Richards and Langthorne theorise, in *Somebody to Love – The Life, Death and Legacy of Freddie Mercury*, that Mercury contracted AIDS in New York in July-August 1982 but wasn't diagnosed HIV+ until autumn 1985. It is certain that the diagnosis became unquestionable in 1987.

From January 1988 to May 1991, Queen worked as often as possible on the tracks that would make up their final three albums. Freddie Mercury quietly succumbed to bronchial pneumonia caused by AIDS on 24 November 1991.

We have lost the greatest and most beloved member of our family. We feel overwhelming grief that he has gone, sadness that he should be cut down at the height of his creativity, but above all great pride in the courageous way that he lived and died. It has been a privilege for us to have shared such magical times.
Queen's official statement, November 1991

'Bohemian Rhapsody' was re-released as a single shortly after Mercury's death. 'These Are the Days of Our Lives', almost unbearably poignant, was the double a-side. The single went to number one in the UK, remaining there for five weeks. Queen's popularity was stimulated in North America when 'Bohemian Rhapsody' was featured in the film *Wayne's World*. The song reached number two in 1992, Queen's biggest hit for twelve years.

The Freddie Mercury Tribute Concert was held in April 1992. Televised to over 1.2 billion viewers worldwide, it raised over £20 million for AIDS charities. Queen's last album featuring Mercury, titled *Made in Heaven*, was released in 1995, four years after his death.

A Kind of Magic (1986)

Personnel:
Freddie Mercury: lead vocals, backing vocals, keyboards, sampler
Brian May: electric guitar, lead vocals, backing vocals, synthesiser, sampler
Roger Taylor: drums, drum machine, backing vocals, synthesiser
John Deacon: bass guitar, electric guitar, synthesiser, sampler, drum machine
+ Spike Edney: keyboards on 'Friends Will Be Friends', 'Don't Lose Your Head';
Joan Armatrading: incidental vocals on 'Don't Lose Your Head'; Steve Gregory:
saxophone on 'One Year of Love'; National Philharmonic Orchestra on 'Who Wants to Live Forever?'.
Recorded between September 1985 and April 1986 at Musicland Studios, Munich;

Mountain Studios, Montreux; Townhouse Studios and Abbey Road Studios, London. Produced by Queen, Mack and David Richards.
UK release date: 2 June 1986. US release date: 3 June 1986.
Highest chart places: UK: 1, USA: 46.

Two months after Live Aid, Queen returned to Musicland in Munich to commence the recording of their twelfth studio album. The single 'One Vision' dates from the first sessions and was released in November 1985. The rest of the album began life as the soundtrack to the Russell Mulcahy film *Highlander*. The songs 'A Kind of Magic', 'One Year of Love', 'Who Wants to Live Forever', 'Gimme The Prize (Kurgan's Theme)', 'Don't Lose Your Head' and 'Princes of the Universe' were written for the film after the band had seen twenty minutes of rough footage.

Some tracks on *A Kind of Magic* album are significantly different to those featured in the film. The title track in particular was given a commercial make-over by Freddie Mercury. Mercury's vocal style for *A Kind of Magic*, and for much of his solo album *Mr. Bad Guy* recorded in 1984, is often strident, almost shouting in songs such as 'One Year of Love' and 'Friends Will Be Friends'. In sessions that followed, 1988 to 1991 after Mercury's diagnosis was confirmed and he quit smoking, his singing is much subtler and more intimate.

For *A Kind of Magic* co-producer Reinhold Mack was joined by David Richards, resident engineer at Mountain and an important part of Queen's last four albums.

Like every Queen album since Jazz, A Kind of Magic was a so-so album, cleverly loaded with two or three potential hit singles.
Mark Blake, *Is This the Real Life?*, 2010

'One Vision' (Queen)

Released as a single a-side, 4 November 1985, and on the 2011 re-release of *A Kind of Magic*. UK: 7. US: 61.
'One Vision' was the second song credited to all four members of Queen. 'It's not often that we really wrote a song together,' says Brian May, 'but this is a good example. We all pitched in and produced ideas.' [1]

Based on lyrics by Taylor, Queen's first new release since their appearance at Live Aid was one of their strongest songs for years. Its powerful opening would ensure placement as the first song of the set for their final tour in 1986, and on live dates with both Paul Rodgers and Adam Lambert.

A documentary recorded during the sessions for 'One Vision' sees Mercury, May and Taylor working on new lyrics – the sparkle in Freddie's eyes as the lyrics come together is a joy to see. This didn't stop him improvising new lyrics for the benefit of the cameras and to the delight of his bandmates: 'one shrimp, one prawn, one clam, one chicken / one heart, one soul, one sex position / one dump, one turd, two tits, John Deacon'.

'One Vision' is effortlessly commercial, whilst simultaneously having loud guitars, a strutting vocal, some reversed masking (Freddie singing 'God works in mysterious ways ...') and a Brian May solo including the tapping technique for the first time since 'It's Late' in 1977.

The single edit, available on *Greatest Hits II*, shortens the introduction and removes about 30 seconds from the end. The b-side is a remix ('Blurred Vision'). There is an extended remix on the 12' single, and on the 2011 re-release of *A Kind of Magic*. *Classic Queen*, released 1992 has the album version with an early fade. Two versions were released as part of *The eYe* video game. One is an edit of the introduction, the other is instrumental.

'A Kind of Magic' (Roger Taylor)
Released as a single a-side, 17 March 1986, b/w 'A Dozen Red Roses for My Darling. UK: 3. US: 42. Also on *Greatest Hits II*, 1991.
One of the songs directly inspired by *Highlander* and the first ever Queen album title track. In *Highlander* the phrase 'a kind of magic' is used by Connor MacLeod (Christopher Lambert) as an explanation of his immortality. There are other references to the film in the lyrics 'one prize, one goal', 'no mortal man', and 'there can be only one'.

The first version, heard at the end of *Highlander*, is a cinematic rock song, heavier than the final version, with a different bass line, sound and structure. This early arrangement is available on the 2011 re-issue of *A Kind of Magic*. 'Freddie got a bee in his bonnet,' comments Brian May. 'He wanted the song to be more catchy. He told us all to bugger off ... "I'll make it a hit". He put the disco beat and changed the bass line, looped parts of my guitar track. He did a great job.' [2]

Freddie said:

> *We all have our own ideas of how a song should be. A song can be done in so many different ways, depending on who's doing it. But sometimes I just feel that it's not right. In the case of Roger's track, which is 'Magic', he did it in a totally different way, which was quite good, but I just felt that there was another commercial streak. I realised that he was going away to LA for about a week so I just got hold of it and I just changed it round completely. And when he came back I said, 'well what do you think?' and he said 'oh, I like it'. Sometimes you can see something else in other people's songs.'* [3]

Mercury's reworking is much more lightweight but fluently commercial. It was Queen's ninth top 3 hit in the UK.

'A Kind of Magic' was performed live on Queen's final tour in 1986 and both with Paul Rodgers and Adam Lambert.

The band's original demo, 'A Kind of Vision', from August 1985 uses the verses, chorus and many of the lyrics from 'A Kind of Magic', but with the phrase 'one vision' used frequently. The words 'a kind of vision' are never used. 'I wrote a bunch of lyrics,' says Roger Taylor, 'a kind of a poem, a Martin Luther King pastiche – and plundered them for both 'A Kind of Magic' and 'One Vision'. [4]

An instrumental version from the 'A Kind of Magic' CD single is called 'A Kind of 'A Kind of Magic''. Two further versions were released in 1996 as part of *The eYe* video game: one is instrumental, the other an extract of Freddie's vocal track. A karaoke mix was released in Japan in 1998.

'One Year of Love' (John Deacon)

This is modern R&B, with heartfelt lyrics. Within Queen, it seems only John Deacon was able to fully articulate his emotional side. 'One Year of Love' features a saxophone solo performed by session musician Steve Gregory, who also played on Wham!'s 'Careless Whisper'. The lush string arrangement heightens the song's romantic message. Freddie's lead vocal is over-strident at times: this is a tender love song, after all.

A longer version was released on a CD with the *Highlander: Immortal Edition* DVD in 2002. This is extended to 6:40 with elements from the original mix.

'Pain is So Close to Pleasure' (Freddie Mercury / John Deacon)

Released as a single a-side, 28 August 1986 (US), b/w 'Don't Lose Your Head'. 'Pain is So Close to Pleasure' was one of the last songs recorded for *A Kind of Magic*, added to the album late in the sessions after the songs for *Highlander* had been completed. It's a neat blend of the funk and disco styles previously heard on songs by Deacon and Mercury, with a touch of Motown swagger. It's easy to imagine Diana Ross singing this song.

'Pain is So Close to Pleasure' was remixed and released as a single in the US, with a different introduction, different balancing of instrumentation and a faster fade-out. This can be heard on the 2011 re-issue of *A Kind of Magic*.

'Friends Will Be Friends' (Freddie Mercury / John Deacon)

Released as a single a-side, 9 June 1986 (UK), b/w 'Seven Seas of Rhye'. UK: 14. Also on *Greatest Hits II*, 1991.

'Friends Will Be Friends' is a piano song, but the simplicity of the construction and performance suggests John Deacon as principle composer. The uncomplicated composition is matched by unusually modest drums and guitar parts – this song is all about getting to that climactic chorus. The effect of a crowd singalong is achieved by varying the backing vocals in each chorus: the first adds just doubletracking to the lead vocal for the title phrases; the second adds vocal harmonies; the third and fourth add backing harmonies to each title phrase and lead guitar figures; Freddie augments the vocal with his trademark high notes and syncopations.

'Friends Will be Friends' was performed live in 1986, sandwiched between 'We Will Rock You' and 'We Are the Champions'.

An excellent extended remix called 'Friends Will Be Friends Will Be Friends...' sounds a lot like Queen of the '70s, with a longer introduction featuring harmonised *a capella* singing, similar to 'Bicycle Race' and instrumental repeats of the chorus where Freddie's piano is more prominent. This was released on the 'A Kind of Magic' CD single, March 1986, on the 'Friends Will Be Friends' 12' single, July 1986 (the same mix, fading out 20 seconds sooner), and on the 2011 re-issue of *A Kind of Magic*.

'Who Wants to Live Forever?' (Brian May)

Released as a single a-side (edited) on 15 September 1986 (UK), b/w 'Killer Queen'. UK: 24. Also on *Greatest Hits II*. Album version released on 12" single, 15 September 1986, b/w 'Killer Queen', 'Forever' and 'Who Wants to Live Forever (single version)'.

One of the best songs Brian ever wrote.
Roger Taylor, commentary on *Absolute Greatest*, 2009.

'Who Wants to Live Forever?' is one of the songs from *Highlander* that has gained significant emotional resonance in light of Mercury's early demise. It is one of Brian May's best songs augmented by a powerful orchestral arrangement. The orchestra was arranged and conducted by Michael Kamen who first came to prominence in the rock and pop field after his work on Pink Floyd's *The Wall* (1979). He became highly sought-after in the 1980s, especially after his scintillating collaboration with Eric Clapton on *Edge of Darkness* (1985). His successes include his work with David Gilmour, Roger Waters, Roger Daltrey, Aerosmith, Tom Petty, Bon Jovi, David Bowie, Bryan Ferry, Eurythmics, Queensrÿche, Rush, Metallica, Def Leppard, Bryan Adams, Coldplay, Sting and Kate Bush, as well as many film soundtracks. Kamen died in 2003, aged 55.

The first verse is sung by Brian May, whose voice, as usual when exposed, sounds thin and reedy. Freddie takes the second verse and the choruses with his usual power and control. May's carefully measured guitar solo, with many fingerpicked notes and very much in the style of Pink Floyd's David Gilmour, is one of his simplest but most dramatic. The song builds to an over-egged climax and final chorus that takes the pomp just a tad too far.

Performed live, superbly, in 1986: monumental and everlasting. In concert, Mercury would sing the whole song and his performances on the 1986 tour were something special – witness the emotion and power in the version from *Live at Wembley '86*. Stripped of the orchestra and choir, the song is transformed into an uplifting and seemingly self-aware acceptance of fate. On the film of the Wembley show, just before this song begins, Freddie says, 'Don't believe those rumours about us splitting up. We're going to be together until we fucking die.'

'Who Wants to Live Forever?' was also included on the tours with Adam Lambert, who sang the song particularly well.

The single mix fades much earlier than the album cut, removing the orchestral ending. A version called 'Forever' was released on 12' single, as a bonus track on the 1986 CD version of *A Kind of Magic* as well as the 2011 re-issue. This is Brian May's piano and synthesiser demo. Understated and delicate, with Freddie's vocal this would have been something to behold. But it's beautiful as it is.

'Gimme The Prize (Kurgan's Theme)' (Brian May)

A satisfactorily meaty rocker from Brian May, using the classic vocals/guitar/ bass/drums line-up, with genuinely powerful vocal performance from Freddie Mercury, just reigning in his tendency to shout. At 2:42, May plays 'guitars as bagpipes' which almost derails the song but mostly sticks to the Eddie Van Halen style so popular in the early 1980s.

Three versions of 'Gimme The Prize (Kurgan's Theme)' were released in 1996 as part of *The eYe* video game: two vocal remixes, one with the dialogue from *Highlander* removed, and an instrumental remix. This instrumental version is also on the 'No One But You (Only the Good Die Young)' CD single released in 1998.

'Don't Lose Your Head' (Roger Taylor)

Released as a single b-side, 28 August 1986 (US), b/w 'Pain is So Close to Pleasure'.

A development of 'A Dozen Red Roses for My Darling' (qv), 'Don't Lose Your Head' was one of the last songs recorded for *A Kind of Magic*. It has a strong lead vocal from Freddie – the lyrics are mostly repeats of the song's four-word title – against an almost totally electronic backing track. The British singer Joan Armatrading features in a vocal cameo.

Released as an instrumental as part of *The eYe*.

'Princes of the Universe' (Freddie Mercury)

Released as a single a-side, 12 March 1986 (US), b/w 'A Dozen Red Roses for My Darling'.

'Princes of the Universe' is a return to the traditional, brawny Queen sound of catchy melodies with bombastic arrangements and a hard rocking edge: ideal as opening music for the *Highlander* film. It was Freddie Mercury's first hard rock song since 'Let Me Entertain You' in 1978.

'Princes of the Universe' was used as the theme for the *Highlander* TV series (1993 to 1999). This no doubt led to the song's inclusion on *Greatest Hits III*, 1999. Released as an instrumental as part of *The eYe*.

Other contemporary songs

'A Dozen Red Roses for My Darling'

Released as a single b-side, 12 March 1986 (US), b/w 'Princes of the Universe'.
Released as a single b-side, 17 March 1986 (UK), b/w 'A Kind of Magic'.
Extended version on 12" single.
'A Dozen Red Roses for My Darling' is an early instrumental version of 'Don't Lose Your Head'.

'Love Makin' Love', 'Coming on Much Too Strong' (aka 'Back to Storm')

Two unfinished Freddie Mercury songs. Both were worked on during the *A Kind of Magic* sessions and there is a demo of 'Love Makin' Love' on *The Solo Collection* and a recording of 'Coming on Much Too Strong' circulates amongst collectors. In both cases it's not clear if available recordings are from 1986 or even whether anyone else in Queen took part.

'You Are the Only One'

A Freddie Mercury song. There is an unreleased demo, just piano and vocals. This may or may not be from 1986 – even if the title might relate to *Highlander*.

'Impromptu'

A semi-improvised funky track recorded at Wembley Stadium, 12 July 1986 and released 26 May 1992 on *Live at Wembley '86*.

'(You're So Square) Baby I Don't Care'

A song by Jerry Leiber and Mike Stoller, recorded by Elvis Presley in 1957. Queen recorded their versions on 21 June 1986, Manheim, released 4 November 2016 on *On Air* (box set version), and at Wembley Stadium, 12 July 1986, released 26 May 1992 on *Live at Wembley '86*.

'Hello Mary Lou (Goodbye Heart)'

The Ricky Nelson song, recorded 21 June 1986, Manheim, released 4 November 2016 on *On Air* (box set version), and at Wembley Stadium, 12 July 1986, released 26 May 1992 on *Live at Wembley '86*. This was a song that Freddie Mercury sang as a teenager at school in India with his band The Hectics.

'Tutti Frutti'

Little Richard's rock & roll classic recorded at Wembley Stadium, 12 July 1986 and released 26 May 1992 on *Live at Wembley '86*.

'Gimme Some Lovin''
Recorded by the Spencer Davis Group in 1966. Queen's version is from Wembley Stadium, 12 July 1986, released 26 May 1992 on *Live at Wembley '86*.

'Big Spender'
Queen often performed this Cy Coleman / Dorothy Fiends song from the musical *Sweet Charity* and made famous by Shirley Bassey. This version was recorded at Wembley Stadium, 12 July 1986, and released 26 May 1992 on *Live at Wembley '86*.

'Looks Like It's Gonna Be a Good Night'
An extemporised tune recorded live on 27 July 1986 at Népstadion, Budapest, Hungary and released on *Hungarian Rhapsody* on 20 September 2012.

'Tavaszi szél vízet áraszt'
A Hungarian children's song performed during the acoustic section of the band's 1986 show in Budapest – Freddie had the words written on his hand. Brian May performed the song in his solo section of the show during Queen + Paul Rodgers' visit to the city in 2008 – he played; the crowd sang.

'Rock in Rio Blues'
Recorded 19 January 1985 in Rio de Janiero. Released as a single b-side, 11 December 1995, b/w 'A Winter's Tale', and on the 2011 re-release of *Made in Heaven*. A harder, bluesy version of the funky vamp released as 'Impromptu' on Live a Wembley '86. This is one of Freddie's vocal improvisations, assisted by piano and lots of reverb and echo and leads into a band improvisation. Vocals and guitar trade off each other in the best Led Zeppelin fashion.

'Theme from New York, New York'
Yes, the Frank Sinatra song. Queen's version was recorded for the soundtrack to *Highlander* and included in the film as a 50-second extract. It's never been officially released.

'I Loved a Butterfly'
A Brian May song, demoed for *A Kind of Magic*, later recorded as 'Some Things That Glitter' on *The Cosmos Rocks* and then, in a simple guitar/vocals arrangement under its original title, on Kerry Ellis' 2010 album *Anthems*, produced by Brian May.

'Battle Scene'
An instrumental, intended for *Highlander*, but not used. It would have sounded great in the film – all atmospheric keyboards and squalling guitar – but out of place on *A Kind of Magic*.

'Love is the Hero'

A Billy Squier song from his album *Enough is Enough* released in September 1986. Although excised from the album cut, Freddie Mercury sings the dramatic opening section and contributes backing vocals to the extended 12" version. Mercury also co-wrote and arranged a second song on this album – 'Lady with a Tenor Sax' – but does not perform on it.

The Miracle (1988)

Personnel:
Freddie Mercury: lead vocals, backing vocals, keyboards, drum machine
Brian May: electric guitar, backing vocals, keyboards
Roger Taylor: drums, backing vocals, percussion, drum machine, keyboards, electric guitar
John Deacon: bass guitar, electric guitar, keyboards
+ David Richards: keyboards on 'I Want It All', 'The Invisible Man' and 'Breakthru', sampler on 'Scandal'.
Recorded January 1988 to February 1989 at Olympic Studios and Townhouse Studios, London, and Mountain Studios, Montreux. Produced by David Richards and Queen.
UK release date: 22 May 1989. US release date: 6 June 1989.
Highest chart places: UK: 1, USA: 24.

1987 was given over to solo projects. Roger Taylor formed The Cross and recorded *Shove It*. Freddie Mercury worked with Montserrat Caballé on the *Barcelona* album and Brian May started five years of intermittent sessions for his first solo album, *Back to the Light*. After eighteen months apart, Queen convened in early 1988 to commence recording *The Miracle*. The finished album was a substantial collection of excellent songs and certainly their best of the '80s. It was the first Queen material to be recorded after Freddie Mercury's diagnosis and represented a dramatic return to form after the five patchy-at-best albums since *Jazz*. At the time there was every expectation that Queen's thirteenth studio album would be their last.

Co-producer David Richards' role in sessions for *The Miracle* was significant. Having spent considerable time with the band during Queen recordings and on various solo ventures, Richards was now a permanent fixture and would remain so through to the sessions for *Made in Heaven*.

By the end of February, after six weeks of sessions, Queen had recorded the basic tracks of over twenty songs. After taking a break for Roger Taylor to tour with The Cross, and for Freddie Mercury to continue his work with Montserrat Caballé, sessions continued in April and May 1988, then July-August 1988, September 1988, November 1988 and January-February 1989.

Originally titled *The Invisible Men* but changed a few weeks before its release date each song is collectively credited to Queen. As was the fashion at the time, some of the songs on *The Miracle* were given extended mixes for 12" singles and CD singles – 'The Invisible Man', 'Breakthru' and 'Scandal'. At one time these – with the B-sides 'Hang on in There', 'Stealin'', 'Hijack My Heart', 'My Life Has Been Saved' and 'Chinese Torture' – were scheduled to be released on an album called *The Alternative Miracle*.

None of the songs on *The Miracle* were performed live by the original Queen line up as Freddie Mercury had retired from touring by the time the songs were written and recorded. 'I Want It All' was, however, performed during the tours with Paul Rodgers (2005-2008) and Adam Lambert (2012-2018).

'Although it's a very techno-aware album, hopefully there's a lot of humanity in there as well,' Brian May said at the time. 'We're enjoying what we're doing, and the sounds reflect us as a group, more than they have done the last few albums. We've played together and evolved things which seemed to excite us, and then built everything around that. I guess when people see *The Miracle* I want them to see the cover, and see four people almost indistinguishable from each other, and I'd like them to feel that inside that wrapper there is a group who has almost the same feeling, it's a very closely-knit group, and we're very much alive, and we're very much out there again.' [5]

'Party' (Freddie Mercury – credited to Queen)
A lively opening to *The Miracle*, with an economic rhythm track and close vocal harmonies leading to a loud instrumental section with octave and three-part guitar harmonies. The segue to 'Khashoggi's Ship' is seamless.

Released as an instrumental as part of *The eYe*.

'Khashoggi's Ship' (Queen)
Another simple, comical rocker, mostly on three chords. The song sounds in E flat, an unlikely key for guitar, so either the guitars have been detuned or the whole recording has been dropped a step. After a section of scat singing the tempo doubles for a live-sounding finale with lots of Freddie's ad-libs.

Released as an instrumental as part of *The eYe*.

'The Miracle' (Freddie Mercury / John Deacon – credited to Queen)
Released as a single a-side, 27 November 1989, b/w 'Stone Cold Crazy (live, 1975)' and 'My Melancholy Blues (live, 1977)'. UK: 21.
One of the highlights of the album: without the layers of synths this could have come straight off *Jazz*. It sounds an awful lot like early '80s ELO in its sound, construction and delivery – it's certainly too lengthy, too complex and far too clever to have been a hit single in 1989.

0:00 Intro – a sharp whack on a hi-hat and pizzicato strings in straight time.
0:05 Verse – the strings underpin Freddie's strong vocals, with an arpeggio
     effect under the word 'miracle'. Drums and piano enter for the second

half and the lead vocal intensifies as the backing drops through the scale in the established ELO pattern.

0:28 Chorus – 'We're having a miracle on earth / mother nature does it all for us / the wonders of this world go on / the hanging Gardens of Babylon / Captain Cook and Cain and Abel / Jimi Hendrix to the Tower of Babel / It's a miracle'. The lead melody for the repeated 'it's a miracle' is three-part harmonised Freddie Mercury. The guitar licks sound reversed – another ELO trick, borrowed from The Beatles.

1:05 Bridge – the song loses its way momentarily as it pushes through chord and tempo changes to reach the next section.

1:21 Guitar solo, with some trademark rising scales and stereo panning (1:25-1:29, see also 'Bohemian Rhapsody') and harmony vocals.

1:36 A short connecting phrase, reminiscent of the later 'The Show Must Go On'.

1:44 Second verse – similar to the first with added guitar flourishes – the backing again harks back strongly to ELO and the Beatles.

2:08 A second chorus – with different lyrics.

2:37 Second guitar solo, played further up the neck and a second bridge, mostly repeated 'it's a miracle'.

3:30 Brian May's third guitar solo – it ends with very 1970s Queen phased block vocal harmonies.

3:48 Coda – Driven by a thrumming bass riff, this is no doubt John Deacon's contribution. The final section 'that time will come' borrows an idea from 'Hey Jude' giving us a new tune, repeated until the end of the song.

Shorter versions are on *Greatest Hits II* (early fade-out) and *Classic Queen* (removes 30 seconds from the middle of the song).

'I Want It All' (Brian May – credited to Queen)

Released as a single a-side, 2 May 1989, b/w 'Hang on in There', on *Greatest Hits II* and on the 2011 re-release of *The Miracle*. UK: 3. US: 50.

A powerful rocker, written about May's relationship with Anita Dobson, who he'd met in 1986 and would marry in 2000. 'The first few weeks of the recording we did a lot of live material, a lot of song ideas came up from jamming,' John Deacon remarked at the time. 'We [also] had a few ideas that were already prepared. 'I Want It All' was one of the few songs that was actually written before we went in.' [6]

'I remember writing most of 'I Want It All' while trying to get weeds out of the lawn.' - Brian May, commentary on *Absolute Greatest*, 2009

Never performed by the classic line-up, 'I Want It All' was included on the Queen+ tours with Paul Rodgers and with Adam Lambert.

The very commercial single mix starts with Queen's trademark harmonies as they sing the chorus vocals – from May's lead guitar onwards this version is similar to the album track, but with May's electric guitar much less prominent and with a strongly pulsing acoustic guitar under the verses. A high keyboard line, in the same tonal range as the guitars, beefs up the choruses. May's solo is edited.

Freddie's vocal is very strong. He adds his own subtle high harmony on the lines 'it ain't much I'm asking', 'move out of my way' and 'for the dreams of youth'. In the bridge the vocals cleverly overlap between May and Mercury:

> May: I'm a man with a one-track mind, so much to do in one life time
> Mercury: People do you hear me?
> May: Not a man for compromise and where's and why's and living lies. So I'm living it all
> Mercury: Yes, I'm living it all
> May: And I'm giving it all
> Mercury: And I'm giving it all, whooooaaaaaah! Yeah! Ahahaaa! Yeah yeeeeeaaaaah!

The 1991 reissue of *The Miracle* includes a unique mix, with the second chorus missing and many different balances of instruments and vocals. Released as an instrumental as part of *The eYe*. A hybrid version released on *Queen Rocks* in November 1997 starts with chorus vocals from the single version and then follows the album version arrangement with the full guitar solo.

'The Invisible Man' (Roger Taylor – credited to Queen)
Released as a single a-side, 7 August 1989, b/w 'Hijack My Heart'. UK: 12. Also on *Greatest Hits II*, 1991.
A first-rate update of the funky sounds heard on *Hot Space*, with a driving, bubbling sequenced bass mostly on one note. The track has a light, humorous touch and very little Brian May outside a squalling twenty-second guitar solo. 'The Invisible Man' was the third single from *The Miracle* and just missed the UK top ten after 'I Want It All' and 'Breakthru' were big hits earlier in the year. Each of the band gets a moment in the spotlight … 'Roger Taylor!'

An early demo version from August 1988 with Roger Taylor's guide vocal was released on the 2011 re-release of *The Miracle*. An extended version is on 12" single and on the 1989 and 2011 CD releases of *The Miracle*.

'Breakthru' (Freddie Mercury / Roger Taylor – credited to Queen)
Released as a single a-side, 19 June 1989, b/w 'Stealin''. UK: 7. Also on *Greatest Hits II*, 1991.
A pop song, written by Taylor, with a jazzy intro, once an entirely separate song, written by Mercury, called 'A New Life is Born'. It starts with unaccompanied voices, with piano joining. The tight harmonies are brilliantly arranged: this could only be Freddie Mercury's work. The verses are effortlessly commercial, and the chorus is wonderfully uplifting – 'If I could only reach you, if I could only make you smile!'

The arrangement is tight and dynamic with some hints at older Queen songs, especially in May's guitar solo, with ascending scales in triplets ('White Queen (As It Began)' and many others) and left/right panning ('The Millionaire Waltz' and 'Killer Queen'). John Deacon even gets a short bass solo in the instrumental bridge with three repeated notes over the synth bass hook.

The song ends with the flanged title phrase.

A longer mix from the 12" single and CD single has a different introduction and has been remixed. Released as an instrumental as part of *The eYe*.

'Rain Must Fall' (Freddie Mercury / John Deacon – credited to Queen)

Probably the least memorable song on *The Miracle*, 'Rain Must Fall' is a funked up calypso written by Freddie Mercury and John Deacon – the verse is more than a little reminiscent of Kelly Marie's 1980 hit single 'Feels Like I'm In Love'.

Even on the beach-bar calypso of 'Rain Must Fall', [Brian] May played like a man trying to blow the song up from the inside.
Mark Blake, *Is This the Real Life?*, 2010

'Scandal' (Brian May – credited to Queen)

Released as a single a-side, 9 October 1989, b/w 'My Life Has Been Saved'. UK: 25.

This is the one song on *The Miracle* album that sounds like the 'old' Queen: a simple, catchy vocal hook with a melodic, Gilmouresque guitar solo based on the vocal melody. Freddie's passionate lead vocal in the verses uses his typical free phrasing often against the beat. There is no chorus, however – the telling final phrase 'Today the headlines tomorrow hard times / And no-one ever really knows the truth from the lies / And in the end the story deeper must hide / Deeper and deeper and deeper inside' was written by May about his treatment by the press over his relationship with Anita Dobson.

An extended mix with louder guitar and percussion is on the 12" single and on the 1991 re-release of *The Miracle*.

'My Baby Does Me' (Freddie Mercury / John Deacon)

Freddie and John try late night soul – it's sexy and sassy and is another of those songs that should sound nothing like Queen. Despite this, or perhaps because of it, 'My Baby Does Me' is one of the most pleasing tunes on *The Miracle*. Brian May channels Carlos Santana in his lead guitar, to great effect.

'Was It All Worth It?' (Freddie Mercury – credited to Queen)

It's easy to forget that Queen's famous valedictory songs, 'The Show Must Go On' and 'These Are the Days of Our Lives' were written by Brian May and Roger Taylor respectively. 'Was It All Worth it?' seems to offer Freddie Mercury's own farewell to his fans, listing his achievements against his challenges and weighing up the balance. 'What is there left for me to do in this life? / Did I achieve what I had set in my sights? / Am I a happy man, or is this sinking sand? / Was it all worth it, was it all worth it?'

Combining a tough guitar riff, with a bubbling bass, a tinkling keyboard, a splash of nonsense orchestration and a stellar ascending, harmonised, chromatic guitar solo, 'Was It All Worth It?' is one of those classic Queen album tracks that lifts their work above pop hits, bombast and stadium chants.

'We served a purpose, like a bloody circus', Mercury sings, with tongue very much in cheek. And, in the final reckoning, Freddie cackles 'Yes, it was a worthwhile experience!'

A reprise of that monster riff and a short fanfare brings the song, and the album, to a close. It's perfectly feasible that when it was recorded 'Was It All Worth It?' was seen as the last song on the last Queen album. Remember them this way.

An instrumental version and an edit of the introduction were released as part of *The eYe* video game.

'A glorious elegy to a life mis-spent.' wrote Stevie Chick in *The Guardian* in November 2014.

Other contemporary songs
'Hang on in There'
Released as single b-side, 2 May 1989, b/w 'I Want It All', as a bonus track on the CD version of *The Miracle*, and on the 2011 re-release of *The Miracle*. The single version fades out a few seconds early, losing the final chord. 'Hang on in There' is a routine song saved by a strong Freddie vocal and some nifty playing in the break-down, including some almost King Crimson-like tempo changes. An edited version, just the introduction, was released as part of *The eYe* video game.

'Stealin''
The bluesy, folky, wonderfully playful 'Stealin'' was released as a single b-side, 19 June 1989, b/w 'Breakthru', and on the 2011 re-release of *The Miracle*.

'Hijack My Heart'
Released as a single b-side, 7 August 1989, b/w 'The Invisible Man', and on the 2011 re-release of *The Miracle*. A Roger Taylor song, up to his usual high standards musically but with very shallow lyrics ('Stuck in the traffic, stuck at the lights, what do I see? / Some stupid bimbo in a fast car next to me').

'My Life Has Been Saved'
Released as a single b-side, 9 October 1989, b/w 'Scandal', and on the 2011 re-release of *Made in Heaven*. This is the original guitar-based version, quite

different to the reworking from a few years later. It's not particularly inspired.

'Chinese Torture'
A bonus track on CD versions of *The Miracle*. Also released on the 2011 re-issue of *The Miracle*. This track was developed as part of May's guitar solo during the last concerts of the Magic Tour. He also included it in his solos with Queen + Paul Rodgers in 2005 and 2006.

'Dog with a Bone', 'A New Life is Born', 'Fiddley Jam', 'I Guess We're Falling Out', 'Brother of Mine'
Titles of songs known or rumoured to have been demoed for *The Miracle*. 'Dog with a Bone' is a one-off bluesy jam session, not meant to be taken seriously. Parts of 'A New Life is Born' were worked into 'Breakthru'; 'Fiddley Jam' eventually became 'Hang on in There'; 'I Guess We're Falling Out' is a Brian May song, perhaps too vitriolic for Queen; 'Brother of Mine' is unheard.

'Face it Alone', 'Affairs', 'Grand Dame'
Three songs worked on in sessions for *The Miracle*, and again for *Innuendo*, but all remain unreleased. 'Face It Alone' is a slow-burning track, one of the gems of the unreleased catalogue with stinging lead guitar and a typically vigorous vocal from Freddie. 'Affairs' is advanced, with verses and choruses in place, but with an incomplete lyric. 'Grande Dame' is an instrumental, little more than studio jamming but showing promise at an early stage of development.

Innuendo (1991)
Personnel:
Freddie Mercury: lead vocals, backing vocals, keyboards, drum machine
Brian May: electric guitar, acoustic guitar, backing vocals, keyboards, drum machine
Roger Taylor: drums, backing vocals, percussion, keyboards, drum machine
John Deacon: bass guitar
+ Steve Howe: Spanish guitar on 'Innuendo'; Michael Moran: keyboards on 'All God's People'; David Richards: keyboards on 'I Can't Live with You' and 'These are the Days of Our Lives'.
Recorded between March 1989 and November 1990 at Metropolis Studios, London, and Mountain Studios, Montreux. Produced by David Richards and Queen.
UK release date: 4 February 1991. US release date: 4 February 1991.
Highest chart places: UK: 1, USA: 30.

Sessions for *Innuendo*, Queen's ruminative and dark last studio album as a functioning four-piece, followed hard upon those for *The Miracle*. With a schedule of three weeks in the studio, followed by two weeks' break, they recorded throughout 1989 and 1990, as Freddie's health and promotional duties for *The Miracle* permitted.

'Freddie wanted his life to be as normal as possible,' Brian May told *The Telegraph* in April 2018. 'He obviously was in a lot of pain and discomfort. For him the studio was an oasis, a place where life was just the same as it always had been. He loved making music, he lived for it.'

'This is hard to explain to people, but it wasn't sad, it was very happy,' notes engineer Justin Shirley-Smith. 'He was one of the funniest people I ever encountered. I was laughing most of the time, with him. Freddie was saying [of his illness] "Fuck that. I'm not going to think about it, I'm going to do this." We all were.'

After ten years of writing and recording singles and album filler, *Innuendo* was developed as a unified whole. The idea of the all-important hit single was pushed back. Even then, two of the songs on *Innuendo* would top the UK charts.

This time, the concept of a magnificent, grandiose, elegant album of great songs was paramount. Certain songs on *Innuendo* are clearly written in the knowledge that Freddie's battle for life is nearing the end. It is difficult to accept that the extraordinary voice behind 'Innuendo', 'Headlong', 'All God's People' and especially 'The Show Must Go On' and 'Don't Try So Hard' could have been recorded by a man who was so physically weak that he could barely stand up. 'Despite his failing health,' writes Phil Chapman, 'Freddie approached the work in hand with an unflinching stoicism and delivered some stunning vocal performances, with remarkable levels of purity and power.' [7]

Reading between the lines, death is a recurring theme on *Innuendo*. Whilst 'Was It All Worth It?' hinted at it, this album deals with the subject more directly, not only in 'These Are the Days of Our Lives' and 'The Show Must Go On' but also indirectly on 'The Hitman' ('Waste that brother'), 'Bijou' ('You and me are destined … to spend the rest of our lives with each other') and 'Don't Try So Hard' ('Just savour every mouthful / And treasure every moment').

For the only time on a Queen album, Brian May plays a guitar solo on every song: some of his best playing can be heard on 'I'm Going Slightly Mad', 'Bijou' and 'These Are the Days of Our Lives'.

Innuendo was released to very positive reviews in the UK, and, remarkably, yielded a straight-in-at-number-one, six-and-a-half-minute, Led-Zeppelin-meets-progressive-rock-and-flamenco hit single. Nine months after the album was released, Freddie Mercury would be dead.

23 November 1991: 'Following the enormous conjecture in the press over the last two weeks, I wish to confirm that I have been tested HIV positive and have AIDS. I felt it correct to keep this information private to date in order to protect the privacy of those around me. However, the time has come for my friends and fans to know the truth, and I hope that everyone will join with me, my doctors, and all those worldwide in the fight against this terrible disease.'

The following day, Freddie Mercury died at approximately 6:48 PM GMT. A week later, a shell-shocked Brian and Roger appeared on *Good Morning Britain* promising a tribute to their department band-member, colleague and friend. A star-studded tribute concert would take place a few months later. For now, there was *Innuendo* and the band's extensive back catalogue.

None of the songs on *Innuendo* were performed live by the original Queen line up. 'The Show Must Go On' and 'These are the Days of Our Lives' were, however, performed during tours with Paul Rodgers in 2005-2008 and Adam Lambert between 2012 and 2018; 'Bijou' was performed in 2008.

'Innuendo' (Freddie Mercury / Roger Taylor – credited to Queen)

Released as a single a-side,14 January 1991, b/w 'Bijou', UK: 1. Also on *Greatest Hits II*, 1991.

Queen's final masterpiece, 'Innuendo' was a most unusual hit single: six minutes in length with many changes of metre, style and dynamic. Even after twenty years, Queen had the capacity to surprise.

There are many resonances of classic Queen of the early 1970s, with power chords, multi-tracked harmony vocals and Freddie's splendid lead vocals. And a Spanish guitar interlude. 'Innuendo' can sit comfortably with Queen's other extravagant hit singles: 'Under Pressure', 'Bicycle Race' and 'Bohemian Rhapsody'. It went straight to no. 1 on 20 January 1991, the week after its release. 'It may have been a challenge to radio programmers,' writes Mark Blake, 'but for Queen fans of a vintage stripe, 'Innuendo' had gratifying echoes of *A Night at the Opera*.' [8]

Probably developing from an unfinished song called 'Assassin', developed in a jam session between May, Taylor and Deacon, Queen's last epic was originally recorded with a Roger Taylor guide vocal. 'Innuendo' is also one of just three songs on the album with only acoustic drums: most of the others have programmed and synth-generated percussion. The exceptions are 'Don't Try So Hard' and 'The Show Must Go On'.

0:00 The taut introduction has drum rolls, deep bass notes and guitar feedback. Something big is on the horizon. The tension is released by power chords and 'ooh-ooh' vocals.

0:46 First verse – the apocalyptic lyrics paint a bleak picture - 'While the sun hangs in the sky and the desert has sand / While the waves crash in the sea and meet the land …'

1:13 Chorus – syncopated bass and guitar – uplifting with quite astonishing singing from Freddie – dropping down to a reprise of the third part of the introduction.

1:49 Second verse – Freddie is on fine voice here.

2:15 Chorus – The descending solo fill with step-wise ornamentation is very Brian May (see also 'Bohemian Rhapsody' and 'You Don't Fool Me'). The song almost stops as we move to a quieter central section.

2:39 A Spanish guitar interlude. The feel takes us right back to the opening moments of 'It's Late' from fourteen years before. There is a horrible forced rhyme – 'Through the sorrow, all through our splendour / Don't take offence at my innuendo.'

3:15 A flamenco section, with handclaps under several overdubbed nylon-strung guitars, some in harmony and all presumably played by Brian May.

3:40 The Spanish guitar solo, played by Steve Howe of Yes.

[They said] 'We want some crazy Spanish guitar flying around over the top. Improvise!' I started noodling around on the guitar, and it was pretty tough. After a couple of hours, I thought: 'I've bitten off more than I can chew here'. I had to learn a bit of the structure, work out what the chordal roots were, where you had to fall if you did a mad run in the distance; you have to know where you're going. But we doodled and I'd noodled, and it turned out to be really good fun.
Steve Howe, *Prog magazine*, 2012

3:55 The 'operatic' section – 'you can be anything you want to be', The time signatures here are unusual – more a feature of progressive rock of the 1970s, not number one hits of the 1990s.

4:17 Electric guitar solo – starting with the same tune as the flamenco section, the first phrase has single tracked lead guitar, the second adds a harmony guitar below that, and the third has an additional, soaring lead guitar line. It's terrific and far too short.

4:52 A reprise of the introduction.

5:03 The third verse – Freddie's barely audible 'ha!' after 'if there's a reason to live or die' is unnerving.

5:29 The final chorus has the prophetic lyrics 'whatever will be will be, we'll just keep on trying' backed by with tumbling block harmonies and loud guitar feedback to fade.

'Innuendo' is an out and out masterpiece – the final forty seconds of must sit alongside Queen's very best musical moments.

The 'Explosive Version' released on 12' and CD single features an explosion after Mercury sings the line 'until the end of time' at 6:14. A heavily edited 'promo version' reduces the song to 3:28 – it loses none of its power despite some harsh transitions. An alternative take of the original vocal track was used in the opening number of the Queen musical *We Will Rock You*. This can be heard on *We Will Rock You: The Musical – Original London Cast Recording*, released in 2002.

'I'm Going Slightly Mad' (Freddie Mercury – credited to Queen)
Released as a single a-side, 4 March 1991, b/w 'The Hitman'. UK: 22. Also on *Greatest Hits II*, 1991.

*A perfectly understated vocal turn from Freddie Mercury highlights this
gentle little pop song, as does one of Brian May's coolest solos: a bit of
slide guitar that unfurls and spirals off in about six different directions at
once.*
Robert Ham, Radio.com, November 2014

A late, silly return to the high camp music hall of 'Good Old-Fashioned Lover
Boy' and 'Seaside Rendezvous', but much darker in tone and very 1990s in
delivery. We have some classic blocked Mercury harmonies and an excellent
Brian May multi-part slide guitar solo. Considering that Mercury was less than
a year from his death when he wrote it, this is a remarkably humorous, positive
song. The video is bonkers.

*Lambasted at the time for being too twee for its own good, 'I'm Going
Slightly Mad' has, like fine wine and Kylie Minogue, only grown better
with age.*
Martin Power, *The Complete Guide to the Music of Queen*, 2006

The LP mix removes 15 seconds from the CD version. Released as an
instrumental as part of *The eYe*. A 'Mad Mix' was released on the 2011 re-issue
of *Innuendo*.

'Headlong' (Brian May – credited to Queen)
Released as a single a-side (US), 14 January 1991, b/w 'All God's People'.
Released as a single a-side (UK), 13 May 1991, b/w 'All God's People'. UK: 14.
Also on *Greatest Hits II*.
Originally written for Brian May's work-in-progress solo album. Brian's demo,
from mid-1990, doesn't yet have the chorus: all instruments and vocals by May.
A second demo has Freddie's vocals and Brian backing up.
   'Headlong' is a relatively hard rock song which might have sounded great on
stage. The rhythm guitar sticks to power chords in the drop-D tuning, just like
'Fat Bottomed Girls'. Freddie's lead vocal is strong and confident.
   The single edit is a punchier mix with some edits. Released as an
instrumental as part of *The eYe*. An almost-complete version but with Brian
May's lead vocals ('embryo with guide vocal') was released on the 2011 re-issue
of *Innuendo*. A US radio edit cuts 45 seconds from the album version.

'I Can't Live Without You' (Brian May – credited to Queen)
'I Can't Live Without You' is a standard Brian May rocker – one of many
liberally dotted through the Queen catalogue. The lyrics, however, delve a bit
deeper than usual: 'I'm having a hard time / I'm walking a fine line between
hope and despair'. We also have perhaps the most contrived rhyme in any
Queen song: 'Lover turns to hater / On this escalator'.
   Like 'Headlong', 'I Can't Live Without You' was originally written for Brian

May's work-in-progress solo album.

The released version includes May's programmed drums, with Roger Taylor providing backing vocals only. The *Queen Rocks* 'Rocks Re-take', version restores Taylor's original drum track and adds some newly recorded guitar and a big ending (rather than fading out). A tight, loud and frankly better 'Brian Malouf Mix' with some different vocals from Freddie and re-programmed drums was released as a promo single in the US in May 1991. A mostly instrumental version which extends beyond the usual fade out was released as part of *The eYe* video game.

'Don't Try So Hard' (Freddie Mercury – credited to Queen)

This powerful, moving, ethereal ballad, mostly sung in falsetto, has some astounding vocal gymnastics in the choruses – the final section pushes the rhythm and Freddie's singing is truly astonishing. Here, again, is a stunning late period Queen song that suggests that even knowing what he was facing, the unfairness of life painfully apparent to him, Freddie Mercury had the strength to leave this gift for anyone who has ever doubted themselves.

The LP mix removes 10 seconds from the CD version, fading early. An edited version was released as part of *The eYe* video game.

'Ride the Wild Wind' (Roger Taylor – credited to Queen)

This is very much a Roger Taylor song – an up-tempo update to 'I'm In Love with My Car'. The arrangement is dominated by guitar, bass, a bubbling synthesiser and what sounds like a drum loop. There are no guitar harmonies and only a very few vocal tricks: just a Queenesque harmony vocal in the third chorus.

An early version with Taylor's guide vocal is on the 2011 re-issue of *Innuendo*. Released as an instrumental as part of *The eYe*.

'All God's People' (Freddie Mercury / Mike Moran – credited to Queen / Mike Moran)

Released as a single b-side, 13 May 1991, b/w 'Headlong'

'All God's People' was developed out of a song called 'Africa By Night' from the *Barcelona* sessions, hence the co-writing credit for Mike 'Rock Bottom' Moran. Notwithstanding the power of its central message, the lop-sided beat, rolling piano and shouty vocals might have fitted amongst the over-the-top arrangements on *Barcelona* but it make it an odd fit on *Innuendo*.

The LP mix removes 26 seconds from the CD version, fading early.

'These Are the Days of Our Lives' (Roger Taylor – credited to Queen)

Released as a single a-side, 5 September 1991 (US), b/w 'Bijou', and 2 December 1991 (UK), b/w 'Bohemian Rhapsody'. UK: 1. US: 2. Also released on *Greatest Hits III*, 1999.

One of Queen's greatest songs, without a doubt. It's a simple verse-chorus-verse-chorus pop-ballad with very rose-tinted lyrics ('These are the days of our lives / They've flown in the swiftness of time / These days are all gone now but some things remain / When I look, and I find – no change'). The backing track is mostly Mercury's, Taylor's and Richards' synthesisers, with a light touch on bass and drums. Brian May plays strummed and arpeggiated chords, lead fills, and slow scales in a variety of styles, as well as a long and very melodic solo. Freddie uses his lower registers throughout. The video, Freddie's last, is heart-breaking.

Performed on tours with Paul Rodgers and Adam Lambert. The LP mix removes 14 seconds from the CD version, lopping off the introduction.

'Delilah' (Freddie Mercury – credited to Queen)

In which Freddie takes us all for a ride in what might his least impressive song. 'Delilah' was the first song recorded for *Innuendo*, with a demo dating from spring 1989. It's dominated by monotonous pumping synth and synth drums, with a few piano overdubs and has a truly silly lyric about Fred's pet cat – 'You make me so very happy when you cuddle up and go to sleep beside me / And then you make me slightly mad when you pee all over my Chippendale suite. Ooh ooh Delilah'.

Brian uses a wah-wah pedal at 2:25 to imitate Delilah's cry. [9]

It's fun, I guess. Perhaps they should have called it 'I'm In Love with My Cat'.

'The Hitman' (Freddie Mercury / Brian May / Roger Taylor – credited to Queen)

Released as a single b-side, 4 March 1991, b/w 'I'm Going Slightly Mad'
Very loud, Metallica-style heavy metal, a long way from the '70s sounds of Black Sabbath and Deep Purple heard on *Queen* and *Queen II*. It would have sounded great live, but here it's metal-by-numbers.

The LP mix removes over a minute from the CD version, editing some of the instrumental sections. An instrumental version of the song was released as part of *The eYe* video game.

'Bijou' (Freddie Mercury / Brian May – credited to Queen)

Released as a single b-side, 14 January 1991 (UK), b/w 'Innuendo'. Released as a single b-side, 5 September 1991 (US), b/w 'These Are the Days of our Lives'.
One of Queen's very best pieces, with some stunning guitar work from Brian May – inventive, passionate, delicate, emotional. 'Bijou' demonstrates a supreme technician at work: each note carefully placed, nothing overdone, no playing for playing's sake. There are echoes of Jeff Beck in May's tone and touch: listen to 'Where Were You' from Beck's *Guitar Shop*

album released in 1989.

The timing of Mercury's vocal entry is perfect: 'you and me, we are destined you'll agree, to spend the rest of our lives with each other'.

'Bijou' was performed live during the 2008 *Cosmos Rocks* tour, with pre-recorded vocals by Freddie Mercury.

The LP mix chops 'Bijou' to 1:17 removing most of May's guitar solo. An edited version was released as part of *The eYe* video game.

'The Show Must Go On' (Brian May – credited to Queen)

Released as a single a-side, 14 October 1991 (UK), b/w 'Keep Yourself Alive'. UK: 16. The CD single included the album versions of 'Now I'm Here', 'Fat Bottomed Girls' and 'Las Palabras De Amor'. The 12" included the album version of 'Body Language'. Released as a single a-side, 6 February 1992 (US), b/w 'Bohemian Rhapsody'.

Queen's final anthem is defiant and heart-breaking in equal measures. 'I don't really think about death,' Freddie said to David Wigg in 1985. '… when I'm dead are they going to remember me? I don't really think about it. When I'm dead, who cares? I don't.'

'Even as he was dying, Mercury threw himself into his majestic, operatic singing,' notes *Rolling Stone*. 'Brian May recalls that Mercury could hardly walk when the band recorded 'The Show Must Go On' in 1990. 'I said, "Fred, I don't know if this is going to be possible to sing",' May says. 'And he went, "I'll fucking do it, darling" – vodka down – and went in and killed it, completely lacerated that vocal.' [10]

'The Show Must Go On' opens with a synth-string pattern with suspended chords similar to the main hook of 'Scandal', presumably transcribed from May's guitar strumming. 'That sequence just got thrust into my head playing around with Roger,' wrote May on brianmay.com. 'I will never know where it came from, but it completely took me over for a long time while the song was in development.'

'The Show Must Go On' uses Freddie's low voice in the verse ('Empty spaces, what are we living for?') but allows him to push to the top of his considerable range in the chorus – the phrase 'I'll face it with a grin, I'm never giving in, on with the show!' is scintillating. The arrangement ends with drum-rolls, arpeggios and guitar trills, reminiscent of 'God Save The Queen'.

'The Show Must Go On' was first performed at the Freddie Mercury Tribute Concert in 1992, with Elton John, then again with Elton John in 1997 – John Deacon's last live appearance with Queen – and on tours with Paul Rodgers (bluesy, solid, full of character) and Adam Lambert (histrionic, limp, empty).

Greatest Hits II has an early fade out. Released as an instrumental as part of *The eYe*. Celine Dion's cover version from 2016 shows just how restrained and subtle Freddie Mercury could be as a singer.

Other contemporary songs
'Lost Opportunity'
Released on a CD single, 4 March 1991, b/w 'I'm Going Slightly Mad' and 'The Hitman'. Also released on the 2011 re-issue of *Innuendo*. This song was recorded in early 1991, the first results of the final batch of Queen recording sessions. It's a lovely, slow, bluesy song sung by Brian May.

'Robbery', 'Self-Made Man', 'My Secret Fantasy'
Three unreleased tracks from the sessions from *Innuendo*. 'Robbery' is a loud guitar-based rocker, so was probably written by Brian May. Lyrics are sketchy – the tempo and approach are reminiscent of 'I'm Scared' from May's solo album *Back to the Light*. 'Self-Made Man' is likely a collaboration between Brian May and Freddie Mercury: it's mostly synthesiser, guitars and programmed drums and not so far from late-'80s period Yes. May takes lead vocals until Freddie comes in on the bridge. Could have been a keeper. 'My Secret Fantasy' is a funky Freddie track, a little Princesque in tone.

'Freedom Train'
'Freedom Train' is a Roger Taylor song initiated during the *Innuendo* period and recorded for Taylor's *Happiness* album in 1994.

Made in Heaven (1995)
Personnel:
Freddie Mercury: lead vocals, backing vocals, keyboards, drum machine
Brian May: electric guitar, lead vocals, backing vocals, keyboards
Roger Taylor: drums, lead vocals, backing vocals, percussion, keyboards
John Deacon: bass guitar, keyboards, electric guitar
+ Rebecca Leigh-White, Gary Martin, Catherine Porter, Miriam Stockley: backing vocals on 'Let Me Live'; David Richards: keyboards on 'My Life Has Been Saved', 'Too Much Love Will Kill You' and '13'.
Recorded 1980-1995 at Musicland, Munich; the Record Plant, Los Angeles; Mountain Studios, Montreux; Allerton Hill, Windlesham (Brian May's home studio); Cosford Mill, Godalming (Roger Taylor's home studio); and Metropolis Studios, London. Produced by Queen.
UK release date: 6 November 1995. US release date: 7 November 1995.
Highest chart places: UK: 1, USA: 58.

By the time Queen finished recording Innuendo in late 1990, Freddie Mercury had been several years HIV+ and was fully aware that he was on borrowed time. He bought an apartment in Montreux to be close to Queen's Mountain Studios, to keep working as his health permitted. In mid-January 1991 the band worked on the song 'Lost Opportunity', the b-side to 'I'm Going Slightly

Mad' recorded in a single session. Four further weeks of sessions in spring yielded 'You Don't Fool Me' and 'A Winter's Tale'

The singer kept working right up until May 1991 when he recorded his last vocal, a sober, sombre and terrifically moving collaboration with Brian May called 'Mother Love'. He returned from Montreux to London on 9 November 1991 and decided to cease taking the drugs designed to keep him alive. Trapped in his Kensington house by the British press, Freddie Mercury died on 24 November 1991.

David Wigg (1985): Do you think you're going to get to heaven?
Freddie: No, I don't want to.
Wigg: You don't want to?
Freddie: No, hell's much better. Look at the interesting people that you're going to meet down there.

Mercury was cremated according to the Zoroastrian faith at the West London Crematorium, Kensal Green on 27 November 1991. His ashes were entrusted to Mary Austin who privately transferred them to their – still unknown – resting place. Mary Austin said in 2000: 'He suddenly announced one day 'I know exactly where I want you to put me, but no-one's to know because I don't want anyone to dig me up. I just want to rest in peace.''

Held on 20 April 1992, at the same Wembley Stadium where Queen annihilated everyone at Live Aid fewer than seven years prior, the Freddie Mercury Tribute Concert for AIDS Awareness celebrated Queen's deceased singer in front of 72,000 spectators and initiated the 'Queen +' concept. The concert was broadcast live to 76 countries – a testament to the band's enduring world-wide popularity.

Short sets from Metallica, Extreme, Def Leppard and Guns N' Roses preceded the three remaining members of Queen performing a twenty-plus song set, including two songs written by David Bowie, extracts from two songs by Led Zeppelin and the debut live performances of 'Innuendo', 'The Show Must Go On' and 'These Are the Days of Our Lives'. Guest vocalists included Roger Daltrey, Robert Plant, Paul Young, Seal, Lisa Stansfield, David Bowie, Annie Lennox, George Michael, Elton John, Axl Rose and, yes, Liza Minnelli. Brian May and Roger Taylor mixed the audio for a 1993 VHS release, remastered and re-released on DVD and BluRay in 2013. Two of these songs ('Somebody to Love' and 'These are the Days of Our Lives') were released on the Queen + George Michael EP *Five Live* on 19 April 1993: a UK number one. The performance of 'All the Young Dudes' was released on Mick Ronson's final album *Heaven and Hull* in May 1994.

Brian May put out his solo album *Back to the Light*, recorded over a five-year period, 1988 to 1992, and toured extensively to promote it through to early December 1993. Roger Taylor recorded the album *Happiness?* in his home studio in the final months of 1993 to the beginning of 1994.

The remaining members of Queen started to come back together in late 1993. Over several weeks Taylor and Deacon added new bass and drum parts to existing tracks. Brian May listened to the results in early 1994 after he had finished promoting *Back to the Light*. He deemed them 'truly catastrophic' and retired to his home studio for several weeks to work on the tracks by himself. These sessions lasted through to spring 1994. By autumn 1994, May, Taylor and Deacon would start working together at Metropolis Studios in London and at May's Allerton Hill Studio with sessions stretching into spring 1995.

This final album, beautifully recorded and surprisingly optimistic and life-affirming in tone, stands alongside their other work. The realisation that no-one is invincible after all is a key theme of the songs here. On *Made in Heaven*, finally, it seems, Queen have grown up.

It was a long journey. The object was to make an album that sounded like four guys in a studio. We knew that if we achieved that, then no one would ask any questions. And that's almost what happened. We started off with just scraps of tape. It was a huge job, two years of my life finding a way of developing the songs. Sometimes there was a complete first take vocal, while other times there were no more than three or four lines. It was a labour of love for me, working through the night perhaps on just one line. But if you can listen to, for example, 'I Was Born to Love You' and say that it was a good performance, I'm glad it sounds so, but obviously it couldn't have been.

Brian May to *Guitarist* magazine in July 1998

'It's a Beautiful Day' (Freddie Mercury / John Deacon – credited to Queen)

Recorded in 1980 at Musicland, Munich and October 1993 to September 1995 at Allerton Hill, Cosford Mill and Metropolis Studios.

And Queen lay down the gauntlet to any doubters by taking a semi-improvised Mercury ditty and turning it into an affirmation of life. There are echoes of 'Don't Stop Me Now' in the lines 'It's a beautiful day / The sun is shining / I feel good / And no-one's gonna stop me now.'

Freddie Mercury sings these lines like he had not a care in the world. Which, when they were recorded in 1980, he didn't. The original piano and vocal tracks date from sessions for *The Game*.

Later described as an 'original spontaneous idea' and released on the 2011 re-release of *The Game* it sounds more like a run-though of a half-finished song combined with some piano experimentation. Nevertheless, it's a typically virile performance, with rollicking piano and a joyous vocal. John Deacon added some lovely orchestrations, Brian May provided some guitar harmonies and one of the best latter-day Queen tracks appeared almost out of nowhere.

'Made in Heaven' (Freddie Mercury)

Recorded 1984 at Musicland, Munich and October 1993 to September 1995 at Allerton Hill, Cosford Mill and Metropolis Studios.

The original version of 'Made in Heaven' was recorded for Freddie Mercury's solo album in 1984 and planned for a time as its title track. In its first incarnation it was anchored by a heavy synthesised drum track. A simple swelling keyboard bed supported one of Freddie's most exuberant vocal tracks. It was Mercury's new single when Queen performed at Live Aid.

The reworked version, hindered by the immovable beat from the original recording, is decidedly uninspired – Queen's usually loose-but-tight rhythm section is unable to push the beat beyond a metronomic trudge. Bursts of multi-tracked guitar and a trucker's modulation lift the song in places, but the pedestrian arrangement and the sheer volume of Mercury's 1984-1985 near shout, which pummelled songs such as 'One Year of Love' and 'Friends Will Be Friends', sound out of place against the more recently recorded songs on the album.

Released as an instrumental as part of *The eYe*.

'Let Me Live' (Queen)

Recorded in September 1983 at the Record Plant, Los Angeles and October 1993 to September 1995 at Allerton Hill, Cosford Mill and Metropolis Studios. Released as a single a-side, 17 June 1996, b/w BBC versions of 'My Fairy King', 'Doing All Right' and 'Liar'. UK: 9. Also released on *Greatest Hits III*, 1999.

'Let Me Live' started life as a jam session between Queen and members of Rod Stewart's band at the Record Plant in Los Angeles on 2 September 1983. Planned as a duet between Queen and Rod Stewart, 'Let Me Live' takes its cue from Janis Joplin's '(Take A Little) Piece of My Heart'. The original mix strayed just a little too close to its inspiration and was replaced with a new mix at the eleventh hour. A US promo cassette released ahead of the album includes the original mix.

The finished article is nothing less than a Queen classic, showing that with the right song and arrangement, this band could polish left-overs into diamonds. 'Please let me live', Mercury begs.

Mercury sings the first verse, choruses and Taylor in his usual robust style, takes on the second verse and bridge. May warbles his way through the last verse. The choruses have an uplifting and, yes, life-affirming gospel sound not so far away from 'Somebody to Love'. Remarkable.

'Mother Love' (Freddie Mercury / Brian May)

Recorded April-May 1991 at Mountain Studios, Montreux and October 1993 to September 1995 at Allerton Hill, Cosford Mill and Metropolis Studios.

'Mother Love' is an untypically sombre and moving song from Queen – with Freddie literally just months away from death, his voice has lost none of its expression, none of its power and none of its character: there is just the smallest quiver in his voice in the second verse ('I can't take it if you see me cry / I long for peace before I die'). This is a vocal performance with soul, from a man whose fate has been written but who will not succumb to morbidity.

Freddie sings on the first two verses only; he died before he was able to complete the song.

May noted in April 2018: 'He just kept saying. 'Write me more. Write me stuff. I want to just sing this and do it and when I am gone you can finish it off.' He had no fear, really. We got as far as the penultimate verse and he said, 'I'm not feeling that great, I think I should call it a day now. I'll finish it when I come back, next time.' But, of course, he didn't ever come back to the studio after that. He said, 'Look, I'm going back to London for a while.' It was always 'a while'. Nothing was ever 'the end'.' [11]

The band's backing is restrained, elegant, atypical – all the bombast and pomp has been stripped back. A snippet of one of Freddie's vocal improvisations, recorded at Wembley Stadium in 1986, precedes extracts from 'One Vision' and 'Tie Your Mother Down', a few seconds of every Queen song ever recorded, a sample from a Mercury's pre-Queen version of 'Goin' Back' and the cries of a baby. This last element signifies re-birth and resurrection, a key tenet of Zoroastrianism. Through his songs, twenty years and fifteen albums, Freddie Mercury's spirit and zest for life lives on.

Queen were never known for their subtlety. But with this song, and with the earlier 'These Are the Days of Our Lives', the band were able to address the very real subject of mortality in a dignified, moving and honourable way.

'Here at last, Mercury allows a chink of light to fall on his terrible sadness.' - Q magazine, 1995

An instrumental version of 'Mother Love' was released as part of *The eYe* video game.

'My Life Has Been Saved' (John Deacon – credited to Queen)
Recorded 1988 at Mountain Studios, Montreux and October 1993 to September 1995 at Allerton Hill, Cosford Mill and Metropolis Studios.

Not one of John Deacon's better songs, dating from sessions for *The Miracle* and released as a b-side to 'Scandal' in October 1989. This version takes the same vocal track from 1989 and completely re-records the backing track, with a fuller keyboards-based arrangement. A full-on Queen version of 'In My Defence' might have been a better idea.

'I Was Born to Love You' (Freddie Mercury)
Recorded May 1984 and April 1995 at Musicland, Munich and October 1993 to September 1995 at Allerton Hill, Cosford Mill and Metropolis Studios.

'I Was Born to Love You' was originally recorded for Freddie Mercury's solo album *Mr. Bad Guy*. It was released a single in April 1985 and reached no. 11 a few weeks before at Queen's appearance at Live Aid. A 'piano and vocals' version, just Freddie, recorded at Musicland in May 1984, was released on the

2011 re-release of *Made in Heaven*.

In its original version, 'I Was Born to Love You' was unashamedly hi-energy disco. The Queen version is a buoyant full-on rocker with a sound that harks back to *The Game* and *Flash Gordon*. Harmonic orchestral guitars, multi-layered backing vocals, a drum sound that just lags behind the beat rather than driving it forward and a full-tilt vocal from Freddie make for a typical late '70s / early '80s Queen sound.

The Queen version was a hit single in Japan in 1996 after being used in a TV advert. It was re-issued in 2004 when it was used as the theme for the Japanese TV series *Pride* and the song topped the chart; their biggest Japanese hit by some margin.

'I Was Born to Love You' was performed by Queen + Paul Rodgers on some of their 2005-2006 dates. This was an acoustic version with vocals were shared by Roger Taylor and Brian May. Adam Lambert sang the song, to great effect, in a handful of the Queen + Adam Lambert shows in Japan in 2014 and 2016.

'Heaven for Everyone' (Roger Taylor)

Recorded 1987 at Mountain Studios, Montreux (assumed) and October 1993 to September 1995 at Allerton Hill, Cosford Mill and Metropolis Studios. Released as an a-side, 23 October 1995, b/w 'It's a Beautiful Day (b-side version)'. UK: 2. Also released on *Greatest Hits III* and on the 2011 re-release of *Made in Heaven*.

Released a single two weeks ahead of the album, and therefore the first new Queen music since Mercury's death, 'Heaven for Everyone' is one of Roger Taylor's best songs. It's a ballad which contrasts dishonesty and sham (a 'world of cool deception') with something more humane ('this world could be fed / this world could be fun').

Of course, Queen fans already knew this track from Roger Taylor's album *Shove It*, released in April 1988. During sessions at Mountain Studios for his album, Taylor asked Freddie Mercury to assist with backing vocals on the song. Two versions were recorded, one with Mercury singing lead, and another with Taylor singing lead and Mercury on backing vocals. The UK edition of the album *Shove It* features Mercury's vocal version, while the UK single featured Taylor's.

Mercury's vocals are intimate and closely-miked to great effect, until the last verse where he really belts it out. Although we lose Taylor's lead vocals in the Queen version, we get some tasty guitar playing from Brian May.

The single mix is fifty seconds shorter, losing some of the repeats of 'this could be heaven' at the beginning. Released as an instrumental as part of *The eYe*.

'Too Much Love Will Kill You' (Brian May / Frank Musker / Elizabeth Lamers)

Recorded 1988 at Mountain Studios, Montreux. Released as a single a-side, 25 February 1996, b/w 'We Will Rock You', 'We Are the Champions', and 'Spread

Your Wings'. UK: 15. Also released on *Greatest Hits III*, 1999.

'Too Much Love Will Kill You' was first heard publicly at the Freddie Mercury Tribute concert in 1992, performed by Brian May at the piano. Even then, or especially then, the lines 'I'm just the shadow of the man I used to be / And it seems like there's no way out of this for me' seemed insensitive. Too much love had killed Freddie Mercury in the most heartless way imaginable.

The song had been first recorded during sessions for *The Miracle* in 1988, and even had a place in the album's running order but was dropped due to issues with licensing – May had co-written the song with Frank Musker, a British professional songwriter who had translated Italian lyrics for Zucchero's late '80s hits, and the American jazz vocalist Elizabeth Lamers. Early demos of the song were performed as a duet between May and Lamers. Based on snippets of demos that circulate amongst collectors it's likely that Lamers wrote most of the lyrics. Nevertheless, it's impossible to imagine that Freddie's diagnosis and death (along with May's other personal issues at the time, including the death of his father and his divorce, both in mid-1988) did not colour the meaning to be relevant directly to May and his outward feelings towards these difficult events.

Brian May recorded 'Too Much Love Will Kill You' for his first solo album, using an arrangement very similar to the 1992 live performance. It's a hideously earnest song, with a video that makes your toes curl as May looks directly into the camera with a look that's so very serious to be laughable. The second half of the live version from May's *Live at the Brixton Academy* is much closer to the Queen arrangement.

Made in Heaven gives us the original Queen mix from 1989, with no additional work. Hearing Freddie sing the lines 'Too much love will kill you, if you can't make up your mind. Torn between the lover and the love you leave behind. You're headed for disaster, 'cause you never read the signs' gives a significance and meaning to the song that's impossible to ignore, despite the intent behind the song's original composition.

An edited version was released as part of *The eYe* video game.

'You Don't Fool Me' (Queen)

Recorded April-May 1991 at Mountain Studios, Montreux and October 1993 to September 1995 at Allerton Hill, Cosford Mill and Metropolis Studios. A single edit was released as an a-side, 11 November 1996, b/w 'You Don't Fool Me (album version)'. UK: 17. Also released on *Greatest Hits III*. The album version was released as the b-side to the single edit.

'You Don't Fool Me', the real surprise of this album, has a strong soul groove with a catchy hook, a sensual vocal from Freddie and strong backing vocals from Roger Taylor. Producer David Richards assembled the basic track from snatches of vocals recorded during early 1991, and the rest of Queen added their instruments during sessions in 1995. The result sounds a lot like the funkier songs from *Hot Space* and is beautifully produced and performed.

Brian May, mixed way back, does his best Eric Clapton impression.

The song was, deservedly, a big hit all over the world. The CD single and 12" singles present various dance remixes of 'You Don't Fool Me', first released in Holland, Italy and France in February 1996. These are all inventive reworkings of the track, if not typical listening for the average Queen demographic. The 'BS Project Remix', 'Freddie's Club Mix', 'Freddie's Revenge Dub' and 'Queen for a Day Mix' were released on the US 12" single in September 1996. The 'Sexy Club Mix', 'Dancing Divaz Club Mix' and 'Dancing Divaz Instrumental Club Mix' were released on CD single and European 12" single in November 1996. An instrumental version of the song was released as part of *The eYe* video game.

'A Winter's Tale' (Freddie Mercury – credited to Queen)

Recorded April-May 1991 at Mountain Studios, Montreux and October 1993 to September 1995 at Allerton Hill, Cosford Mill and Metropolis Studios. Released as a single a-side, 11 December 1995, b/w 'Rock in Rio Blues'. UK: 6.

'A Winter's Tale' is a mid-paced ballad. Freddie admires the scene from his window in Montreux, describing what he sees in a shouty vocal. 'Oh, it's bliss,' sings our Fred. No amount of layered backing vocals can polish this above hackwork.

A drier 'cosy fireside mix', which strips the reverb and pushes forward the lead vocal is available on the 2011 re-release of *Made in Heaven*.

'It's a Beautiful Day (Reprise)' (Freddie Mercury / John Deacon – credited to Queen)

Recorded in 1980 at Musicland, Munich and October 1993 to September 1995 at Allerton Hill, Cosford Mill and Metropolis Studios. A single version was released as a b-side, 23 October 1995, b/w 'Heaven for Everyone', and on the 2011 re-issue of *Made in Heaven*.

A reprise of the opening track that manages to be thirty seconds longer as it morphs into a full-on rocker. The up-tempo mid-section is fully-loaded with guitars and drums. It's a genuine Queen classic, so hearing it twice is no hardship.

The single b-side version is very similar to the reprise from the album. Three seconds have been snipped at around 1:25 and rather than 55 seconds of full-on rock after the first 'yeah', we get a cross-fade to Freddie's piano and vocal and reprise of the orchestral opening. This single mix is perhaps a better arrangement than the album versions. 'No-one's gonna stop me now. It's hopeless, so hopeless to even try,' sings Freddie. An instrumental remix was released as part of *The eYe* video game. This contains elements of all three versions from 1995, including Freddie's piano track and 'yeah', and the heavy guitar and drums from the reprise / single mix. A techno remix by Ross Robertson / DJ Koma, was released as a download, 31 October 2005. Do we really need a *fourth* version of this? Yes, we do! This uplifting, up-tempo version combining all the other versions was played over the PA on the Queen + Paul Rodgers 2005-2006 tours as the band was ready to come on stage and was used over the closing credits of the DVD of the tour. It rocks.

'Yeah' (Queen)

Recorded in 1981 at Musicland, Munich.

A four-second extract from the song 'Action This Day' from *Hot Space*, banded as a separate track.

'13' (Queen)

Recorded October 1993 to September 1995 at Allerton Hill, Cosford Mill and Metropolis Studios.

For better or worse, Queen continue to surprise with a 22-minute ambient sound collage, a kind of requiem to Freddie Mercury. Starting with loops of the keyboard track to 'It's a Beautiful Day', '13' ebbs and flows, is beautifully calm and keeps you on your toes with some ghostly laughter. Extraordinary.

This last track, a 22-minute wash of celestial ahhs and twinkle, presents what could be rock's first-ever depiction of the afterlife, with heaven presented as some flouncy Hollywood epic. It's the perfect theatrical epitaph for a life dedicated to gorgeous artifice.
Entertainment Weekly, 1995

Footnotes

[1] commentary on *Absolute Greatest*, 2009.
[2] commentary on *Absolute Greatest*, 2009.
[3] interviewed spring 1986 (*Greatest Video Hits II*).
[4] commentary on *Absolute Greatest*, 2009.
[5] interviewed May 1989 (*Greatest Video Hits II*).
[6] interviewed May 1989 (*Greatest Video Hits II*).
[7] *The Dead Straight Guide to Queen*, 2017.
[8] *Is This the Real Life?*, 2010.
[9] The cat imitation with voice and/or guitar has famous precedents: Rossini's 'Duetto buffo di due gatti' ('Cats Duet', sometimes called 'The Meow Song'), 'The Cat Walk' by Bill Haley and His Comets (1959, guitar by Frank Beecher) and Queen's own 'Killer Queen' (after 'faithful as a pussycat').
[10] December 2010.
[11] *The Telegraph*, April 2018

Epilogue: The Show Must Go On

Who cannot forgive Brian May and Roger Taylor for wanting to continue to play Queen music all over the world? In the years after Freddie Mercury's death they have performed and recorded with many artists as 'Queen + *[insert name here]*', most notably with Paul Rogers and Adam Lambert. And the Muppets.

New Queen songs have appeared on *Queen Rocks*, as part of the 46664 project and *The Cosmos Rocks*. Unfinished songs have been spruced up and released on *Queen Forever*.

Queen Rocks (1997)

Released November 1997: a compilation album with one new song, one modified song ('I Can't Live with You'), unique hybrid versions of two songs ('I'm in Love with My Car', 'I Want It All') and fourteen other Queen tracks from the back catalogue.

'No One But You (Only the Good Die Young)'

Recorded summer 1997 at Allerton Hill and Cosford Mills Studios. Written by Brian May. Released as a single, 5 January 1998, b/w 'Tie Your Mother Down', 'We Will Rock You (Ruined by Rick Rubin)' and 'Gimme The Prize (instrumental mix)'. UK: 13. Also released on *Greatest Hits III*, 1999.

The only new song on *Queen Rocks* didn't rock at all. This mawkish ballad dates from early sessions for Brian May's solo album *Another World*, and purports to celebrate all those who died young. Whilst not dismissing the subject matter, the overall result is, like the earlier 'Too Much Love Will Kill You', over-earnest and faintly embarrassing.

This simple verse-chorus-verse-chorus song, with no guitar solo and no guitar harmonies, has a small place in Queen history as the last release to feature John Deacon. 'As far as we are concerned, this is it,' John Deacon told *Bassist* in April 1996. 'There is no point carrying on. It is impossible to replace Freddie.'

As sung by Kerry Ellis with new backing, 'No One But You (Only the Good Die Young)' was released as a download in 2005 and later the *We Will Rock You – Around the World* EP, credited to Queen + Kerry Ellis. A Spanish version from 2005, sung by Eva Maria is credited to Queen + Eva Maria. The backing track is the same as the Kerry Ellis version.

Greatest Hits III (1999)

With *Greatest Hits* (October 1981) covering the period 1973 to 1980, and *Greatest Hits II* (October 1991) including hits from 1981 to 1991, there wasn't much left in the barrel for a third hits compilation. Five songs from *Made in Heaven* were bolstered by 'These Are the Days of Our Lives', remixes of 'Under Pressure' and 'Another One Bites the Dust', live versions of 'The Show Must Go On' (with Elton John) and 'Somebody to Love' (with George Michael), the Christmas single that nobody bought ('Thank God It's Christmas'), solo songs from Freddie Mercury (Living on my Own', 'The Great Pretender' and 'Barcelona') and Brian May ('Driven by You') and, remarkably, two songs that weren't even big hits, never mind 'greatest' – 'Princes of the Universe' and 'Las Palabras de Amor (The Words of Love)'.

46664 (2003)

There is no doubt that the 46664 series of charity concerts in South Africa and elsewhere promoted a very worthy cause – and one that's close to the hearts of Brian May and Roger Taylor: global HIV/AIDS awareness and prevention.

Queen performed at the inaugural concert on 29 November 2003, performing four new songs.

'Say It's Not True'

'Say It's Not True' is an excellent song – low-key and with a gorgeous chorus. A 2003 studio version has never been released, but a live version is available on the album *46664 – African Prayer.* It was re-recorded for *The Cosmos Rocks.*

'Invincible Hope'

This Roger Taylor song is a major mis-step. It features extracts from Nelson Mandela's speeches, a tired arrangement and a pedestrian chorus. The studio version was available as a download-only track, credited, without shame, to 'Queen + Nelson Mandela', in October 2003. A remix was released in January 2004. A live version, should you want one, was recorded in November 2003 at Green Point Stadium, Cape Town, South Africa and is available on the album *46664 – Long Walk to Freedom.*

'46664 The Call'

Just as you get over disappointment of 'Invincible Hope', Brian May delivers this – surely the worst song ever to bear the Queen name. It mixes the chord sequence from 'The Show Must Go On' with a laughably over-earnest vocal from Brian May. Notwithstanding the underlying message, with which it's impossible to disagree, this really is a stinker of a song. The studio version remains unreleased but was broadcast on radio and can be heard on YouTube, should you wish. A live version was recorded in 29 November 2003 at Green Point Stadium, Cape Town, South Africa and is available on the album *46664 – Long Walk to Freedom.*

'Amandla'

Amandla is a Zulu and Xhosa word meaning 'power'. This up-tempo African-influenced song, which allows a community sing-along in the chorus, was written by Brian May and Dave Stewart to close the first 46664 concerts. The studio version which features Queen, Dave Stewart and Anastacia was released as a download in 2003. A live version with a cast of thousands, was recorded 29 November 2003 at Green Point Stadium, Cape Town, South Africa and is available on the album *46664 – Amandla*.

As a footnote, Taylor and May performed with Zucchero at the 2003 concert. Their recording of the Korgis song 'Everybody's Got to Learn Sometime' was released as a single in Italy in October 2004, credited to Zucchero, Queen and Sharon Corr.

Queen + Paul Rodgers (2005-2008)

The first series of 'Queen +' projects had been unqualified successes, at least commercially. Those with David Bowie (1981), George Michael (1993) and Five (1999) had been number one hits in the UK, and the collaborations with Wyclef Jean (1998) and Vanguard (2003) provided two further entries into the top twenty.

It came as no surprise that May and Taylor would want to extend this success into a live tour. Their collaborator between 2005 and 2008 would be ex-Wildflowers, ex-Free, ex-Bad Company, ex-The Firm, ex-The Law vocalist Paul Rodgers.

There's no doubt that Paul Rodgers is one of the great rock singers. As vocalist in Free (1968-1972) and Bad Company (1973-1982) he sang on many classic tracks including 'All Right Now', 'Wishing Well', 'My Brother Jake', 'Bad Company', 'Feel Like Making Love' and 'Can't Get Enough', all staples of classic rock radio.

Free (with Rodgers) and Smile (with May and Taylor) performed on the same bill in London on 27 February 1969. And in 1975, Queen's management wish list included Peter Grant, manager of both Led Zeppelin and Rodgers' then current band Bad Company. No doubt their paths crossed a few times in the 1970s and 1980s.

Rodgers first worked with Brian May in October 1991, when Rodgers sang 'Now I'm Here' with May at the Expo '92 Concert in Seville. May guested on Rodgers' album *Muddy Water Blues* in 1993, and at some of Rodgers' concerts in 1994 and 1996. Together they released the charity single 'Reaching Out' in 1996. Both appeared at a London concert to celebrate the 50th Anniversary of the Fender Stratocaster guitar in September 2004 and Rodgers performed with both May and Taylor at the inaugural UK Hall of Fame ceremony in November 2004.

May, Taylor and Rodgers performed large tours in 2005-2006 and 2008 billed as Queen + Paul Rodgers. Queen would continue to support 46664, with Q+PR appearances at the 2005 concert in South Africa, and at the 2008 concert in London.

In 2005-2006 the band's set list included only four Freddie Mercury songs: 'Bohemian Rhapsody', 'Crazy Little Thing Called Love', 'Killer Queen' and 'We Are the Champions', and just one by John Deacon, a rockier arrangement of 'I Want to Break Free'. Five songs written by Roger Taylor included the major hits

'A Kind of Magic', 'These Are the Days of Our Lives' (Roger Taylor vocal), 'Radio Ga Ga' (Roger Taylor and Paul Rodgers vocal), the classic 'I'm In Love with My Car' (Roger Taylor vocal) and 'Say It's Not True' (performed in an acoustic version, Roger Taylor vocal). Around half the Queen songs included in the set were written by Brian May: 'Fat Bottomed Girls', 'Hammer to Fall', 'I Want It All', 'Love of My Life' (Brian May vocal), 'The Show Must Go On', "39" (Brian May vocal), 'Tie Your Mother Down' and 'We Will Rock You'. A handful of Paul Rodgers songs completed the set.

The 2008 tour dropped 'Killer Queen' and 'Fat Bottomed Girls' and added 'Another One Bites the Dust', the first live performances of 'Bijou' from *Innuendo* (with pre-recorded vocals from Freddie), and six songs from *The Cosmos Rocks*. And, as in 1986, there was a one-off performance of 'Tavaszi szél vízet áraszt' in Budapest.

Several recordings from both tours were made available as downloads in 2005 and 2008 including many performances and some songs not on the official live albums.

The Cosmos Rocks (2008)

Personnel:
Brian May: guitar, backing and lead vocals, bass, keyboards, piano
Roger Taylor: drums, backing and lead vocals, percussion, keyboards
Paul Rodgers: lead vocals, guitar, bass, keyboards, piano and harmonica.
Recorded between late 2006 and summer 2008 at Roger Taylor's Priory studio, based in his house near Godalming in Surrey.
UK release date: 15 September 2008. US release date: 14 October 2008.
Highest chart places: UK: 5, USA: 47.

'Cosmos Rockin'', 'Small', 'C-lebrity', 'Say It's Not True', 'Surf's Up ... School's Out!', 'Small (reprise)' (Roger Taylor)

'Cosmos Rockin'', once it gets over its pretentions to being son-of-'One Vision', unsurprisingly sounds like Bad Company with Queen's backing vocals – it's harmless and fun, as Queen rockers are, but sorely misses Freddie's tongue-in-cheek delivery. 'Small' is another great song by Roger Taylor, with a simple and genuinely uplifting chorus. Layered with acoustic guitars, and beautifully and tenderly sung by Paul Rodgers using his lower registers rather than his rock bellow, this song is a triumph despite May's out-of-place and over-the-top guitar solo. 'C-lebrity' pokes fun at tabloid culture and mixes a robust Rodgers vocal with a typically droll chorus. Foo Fighters drummer/vocalist Taylor Hawkins guests. It was released as a single a-side, 8 September 2008 (b/w 'Fire and Water' [live in Japan]). UK 33. 'Say It's Not True' is a new recording with a new arrangement. Taylor sings the first verse, May takes the second verse, and Rodgers the third as the song kicks into gear. Brian May does his best to kill the tune with a million guitar overdubs. It was released as a single, 1 December

2007. UK: 90. 'Surf's Up ... School's Out!' takes the riff from 'Now I'm Here' and pumps it up into a bluesy stomper.

'Cosmos Rockin'' and 'C-Lebrity' were performed throughout the 2008 tour. Both were recorded on 12 September 2008 in Freedom Square, Kharkiv, Ukraine, and released on *Live in Ukraine*, 15 June 2009. 'Say It's Not True' was first performed by Queen + Paul Rodgers in 2005, at the third 46664 concert. During 2005 it was an acoustic performance sung by Roger Taylor. Recorded 9 May 2005, Sheffield, released on *Return of the Champions*, 19 September 2005; and 27 October 2005, Japan, released on *The Cosmos Rocks – Limited Edition* (Japan only). In 2008, 'Say It's Not True' was a full band performance sung in turn by Taylor, May and Rodgers. Recorded 12 September 2008 in Freedom Square, Kharkiv, Ukraine, released on *Live in Ukraine*, 15 June 2009. 'Surf's Up... School's Out!' was performed regularly in 2008.

'Time to Shine', 'Warboys', 'Call Me', 'Voodoo', 'Through the Night' (Paul Rodgers)

'Warboys' is trite and stupid, 'Call Me' is refreshing with some lovely early-Queen guitar harmonies but is perhaps too close to a mash-up of 'Can't Get Enough' and 'Crazy Little Thing Called Love'. 'Voodoo' is a forgettable slow blues. 'Through the Night' is very Bad Company in sound and feel – the weak chorus lets down the strong verses and quality of performance.

'Time to Shine' was performed once in concert: in Antwerp on 23 September 2008. 'Warboys' and 'Voodoo' were both first performed on Paul Rodgers' solo tour in 2006, then with Queen a handful of times in 2008.

'Still Burnin'', 'Some Things That Glitter', 'We Believe' (Brian May)

'Still Burnin'' is a strong rocker, very Paul Rodgers in delivery but with shallow 'rock and roll never dies' lyrics. May plays slide guitar with wah-wah and Taylor's drumming echoes the tempo and rhythm of 'We Will Rock You', a nod made more explicit when a sample of the original is dropped into the mix. 'We Believe' is platitude-filled nonsense. 'Some Things That Glitter' is not gold.

'We Believe' was performed on the European and South American tours in 2008.

Other contemporary songs

'Runaway'

The Del Shannon song rearranged as a mid-paced rocker and released as a bonus track on some versions of *Cosmos Rockin'*. A-why, why, why, why, why?

'Take Love (Where You Find It)'

A half-decent song, written by Paul Rodgers in the Bad Company style and performed at most of the dates on the 2006 tour of North America. This was the first collaborative song by Queen + Paul Rodgers but was not taken forward into sessions for *The Cosmos Rocks*.

Other live performances, 2005-2008
These non-Queen songs were also performed during this period.

'Reaching Out'
'Reaching Out' is a song by Don Black – legendary lyricist for many James Bond theme songs and several Lloyd-Webber musicals – and Andy Hill, who has written number one hits for Bucks Fizz and Celine Dion. 'Reaching Out' was a charity single released in July 1996, credited to Rock Therapy – May and Rodgers on guitar and vocals, with contributions from Lulu, Sam Brown, Charlie Watts and Andy Fairweather-Low. May and Rodgers appeared on *Top of the Pops* to promote the song, which stalled outside the UK top 100, despite its noble intent.

Queen + Paul Rogers performed this as the opening song on their 2005 tour; an unexpected but very effective choice. Live versions are on *Return of the Champions* and *The Cosmos Rocks – Limited Edition* (Japan only).

'Wishing Well', 'All Right Now', 'Fire and Water', 'Little Bit of Love', 'The Stealer'
Five songs originally recorded by Free and performed by Queen + Paul Rodgers.

'All Right Now', first released by Free in May 1970, has been released on *Return of the Champions* (2005); *The Cosmos Rocks – Limited Edition* (2008); *Live in Ukraine* (2009). 'Fire and Water', first released by Free in June 1970, was recorded in Hyde Park in 2005 and released as the b-side to 'C-Lebrity' (2008). 'The Stealer', first released by Free in December 1970, was performed once in 2008. 'Little Bit of Love', first released by Free in June 1972, was performed several times in 2005. 'Wishing Well', first released by Free in January 1973, was released on *Return of the Champions* (2005).

'Feel Like Making Love', 'Can't Get Enough', 'Seagull', 'Shooting Star', 'Bad Company', 'Rock & Roll Fantasy'
Six Bad Company songs performed by Queen + Paul Rodgers.

'Can't Get Enough', first released by Bad Company in June 1974, was released on *Return of the Champions* (2005); *The Cosmos Rocks – Limited Edition* (2008). 'Seagull', first released by Bad Company in June 1974, was recorded in Rome on 4 April 2005 for an Italian promo single and is also on *Live in Ukraine* (2009). The song was performed by Rodgers on vocals and acoustic guitar and Taylor on bongos on both Q+PR tours. 'Bad Company' first released by Bad Company in June 1974 is on *Live in Ukraine* (2009). Paul Rodgers played piano during these very robust performances. 'Feel Like Making Love', first released by Bad Company in June 1975, is on *Return of the Champions* (2005); *The Cosmos Rocks – Limited Edition* (2008); *Live in Ukraine* (2009). 'Shooting Star', first released by Bad Company in June 1975, is on *Live in Ukraine* (2009). 'Rock & Roll Fantasy', first released by Bad Company in March 1979, was performed on occasion in 2005 and 2006.

'Let There Be Drums'
A 1961 drums/guitar instrumental composed by Sandy Nelson and Richard Podolor and performed by Taylor and May as part of Taylor's solo spot. It's on *Return of the Champions* (2005).

'Imagine'
John Lennon's 1970 song, performed just once, at Hyde Park on 15 July 2005.

'Last Horizon'
One of Brian May's best guitar-based pieces: emotional, restrained and worth it. It dates from 1988, recorded contemporaneously but not as part of sessions for *The Miracle*, and was released on May's solo album *Back to the Light* in 1992. Often performed in May's solo tours, it was introduced to the Queen + Paul Rodgers setlists, and live performances have been released from 4 April 2005, in Rome, and 5 October 2008 in Hamburg (both as downloads).

Queen Forever (2013)
Another compilation album put together to promote three more grave robberies. Actually, 'Let Me in Your Heart Again' is a classic Queen power ballad, and the 'new' version of 'Love Kills' adds a twist to an old Freddie disco classic. But 'There Must Be More to Life Than This', is necrophilia and nothing less.

Queen Forever is a schizophrenic album which includes some overlooked Queen classics ('It's a Hard Life', 'You're My Best Friend', 'Love of My Life', 'Lily of the Valley', 'Don't Try So Hard', 'Bijou', 'These Are the Days of Our Lives', 'Las Palabras de Amor (The Words of Love)', 'Who Wants to Live Forever'), some hoary old singles that everyone in the world must own by now ('Play the Game', 'Save Me', 'Somebody to Love' and 'Crazy Little Thing Called Love') and four clinkers ('Drowse', 'Long Away', 'A Winter's Tale', 'Too Much Love Will Kill You').

The deluxe edition adds fourteen more great-to-excellent songs: 'Dear Friends', 'You Take My Breath Away', Spread Your Wings', 'Nevermore', 'Friends Will Be Friends', 'Jealousy', 'One Year of Love', '39', 'Mother Love', 'Made in Heaven', 'Is This the World We Created ...?', 'In the Lap of the Gods ... Revisited', and 'Forever'.

Many of these fade early.

Queen + Adam Lambert (since 2011)

If rock music was born on 27 January 1956, matured on 26 May 1967, and hit middle age on 13 July 1985, then it rolled over and died on 3 June 2002 – the 'Party at the Palace'.

Queen played their part. Fifty-five-year-old Brian May performed 'God Save the Queen' on the roof of Buckingham Palace, shoulder-length, permed hair blowing artfully in the breeze, rock 'n' roll waistcoat and bespoke trench coat in place. And, later, three Queen songs were assassinated by May, Taylor, Will Young and the cast of *We Will Rock You*. [1]

Poor Freddie, not twelve years dead and his legacy already in tatters.

After 2002, rock music became retro. Big names of the '70s and '80s toured their back catalogues. Those that were split up, too old or too dead were replaced by tribute bands – the biggest were able to sell out arenas. In parallel, reality TV shows such as *American Idol*, which debuted exactly nine days after the Party at the Palace, pandered to the lowest common denominator, homogenising all musical styles into a flat, loud, sham.

If Queen + Paul Rodgers at least *tried* to come over as a real band playing (some) new music, then May and Taylor's next move was seen by some as shameless exploitation. Their choice of vocalist was Adam Lambert, American idol runner up in 2009. Queen + Adam Lambert have completed several major tours performing a wide range of classic and lesser-known songs from Queen's back catalogue, including 'Keep Yourself Alive', 'Seven Seas of Rhye', 'Killer Queen', 'Now I'm Here', 'Stone Cold Crazy', 'In the Lap of the Gods … Revisited', ''39', 'Love of My Life', 'Bohemian Rhapsody', 'Tie Your Mother Down', 'Somebody to Love', 'We Will Rock You' (both versions), 'We Are The Champions', 'It's Late', 'Spread Your Wings', 'Fat Bottomed Girls', 'Don't Stop Me Now', 'Dragon Attack', 'Another One Bites The Dust', 'Save Me', 'Crazy Little Thing Called Love', 'Under Pressure', 'Radio Ga Ga', 'I Want To Break Free', 'One Vision', 'A Kind of Magic', 'Who Wants To Live Forever?', 'I Want It All', 'These Are the Days of Our Lives', 'The Show Must Go On', 'I Was Born to Love You' and 'Love Kills', amongst others.

Q+AL also performed the Adam Lambert song 'Ghost Town', and a vocal improvisation ('All Your Love Tonight') during 2014-2015, and one or two of Lambert's 'Two Fux' and 'Lucy' and/or the P!nk song 'Whataya Want from Me' in 2017-2018.

All in all, Adam Lambert was a good choice for Queen. He is a consummate professional with passion for the material and the vocal dexterity to hit the notes. But his often shrill, sometimes arch delivery grates to some ears. It's time that May, Taylor and Lambert release some original music of their own.

But, for now, there is no denying that the very popular Queen bandwagon continues to roll all around the world courtesy of what amounts to Queen's greatest tribute band.

The show must go on, it seems.

But let's leave the final word to writer and critic Mark Monahan. [2]

Queen were ... utterly preposterous in every way. Mercury was a cartoonish – and potentially alienating – camp figure; the other three were as boring-looking as can be. Resolutely uncool, their music heaved with pretensions, and their lyrics were often pure nonsense. Queen preferred to sing about fat bottomed girls and the delights of pootling about on bicycles. In short, they seldom if ever tried to 'say' anything. It has ... been the band's very refusal to take things too seriously that has so appealed to the public (while often confounding the more po-faced elements of the music press). Freddie Mercury always admitted that he wanted to pack as much fun into his life as he conceivably could and hang the consequences. His promiscuity caught up with him in the cruellest way, and yet his blazing quest for a good time was also pivotal to the band's success. Even Mercury's charisma would have counted for nothing, though, without his and his colleagues' copper-bottomed musicianship. Mercury tickled the ivories as eloquently as he sang, May and Taylor were talented backing (and occasionally lead) vocalists, and all four of them wrote. The result was the most fabulous and unforgettably melodic collection of songs, with that uniquely lush, instantly recognisable 'Queen sound' running through almost every one. Stylistically, they were glam, but too good to be glam rock; technically brilliant, but too entertaining to be prog rock; hard-rocking, but too joyful to be heavy metal. Nothing seemed to be beyond them. For all his excess, Mercury was a hopelessly appealing, not to mention endearingly private figure whose sexuality and love life were – inconceivable as it now seems – not a matter of public record. Ultimately, though, like all the best bands, Queen had superb parts, but were also much more than their sum. And, although they found recording together so effortless that they privately referred to their studio as 'the sausage factory', the fact is that what they did was not easy at all. Muse, Mika, the Darkness and countless other acts have wisely looked to the band for inspiration. But swipe Queen's ever-lustrous crown? You must be joking.'

Amen, brother.

Footnotes

[1] This is the only mention of that show in this book. ('prolefeed', *The Daily Telegraph*, 2002).

[2] 'Why we still can't get enough of Queen', *The Telegraph*, 30 October 2015.

...and nobody played synthesiser.

Appendices

Bibliography

Blake, M. (ed.), *Queen – The Inside Story* (EMAP Metro, London, 2005)

Blake, M., *Is This the Real Life?* (Da Capo Press, Philadelphia, 2011)

Burrows, T., *Guitar Family Trees* (New Burlington, London, 2007)

Chapman, P., *The Dead Straight Guide to Queen* (Red Planet, Penryhn, 2017)

Christgau, R., *Christgau's Guide – Rock Albums of the 1970s* (Vermilion, London, 1981)

Dimery, R. (general editor), *1001 Albums You Must Hear Before You Die* (Cassell, London, 2005)

Dimery, R. (general editor), *1001 Songs You Must Hear Before You Die* (Cassell, London, 2010)

Evans, D and Minns, D., *Freddie Mercury: This is the Real Life* (Britannia Press, Culver City, 1993)

Freestone, P. with Evans, D., *Freddie Mercury 'An intimate memoir by the man who knew him best'* (Omnibus, London, 2001)

Hince, P., *Queen Unseen* (John Blake Publishing, London, 2011)

Jackson, L., *Brian May – The Definitive Biography* (Portrait Books, London, 2007)

Jackson, L., *Queen – The Definitive Biography* (Piatus, London, 1999)

Jenkins, J. and Gunn, J., *Queen – As It Began* (Sidgwick & Jackson, London, 1992)

Jones, D., *The Eighties: One Day, One Decade* (Windmill Books, London, 2014)

Jones, L-A., *Freddie Mercury – The Definitive Biography* (Hodder & Staughton, London, 2012)

Magee, S., *Desert Island Discs: 70 Years of Castaways* (Bantam Press, London, 2012)

LeMieux, P. and Unger, A., *The Queen Chronology* (Across THE Board Books, Toronto, 2013)

Power, M., *Queen – The Complete Guide to their Music* (Omnibus Press, London, 2006)

Richards, M. & Langthorne, M., *Somebody to Love – The Life, Death and Legacy of Freddie Mercury* (Blink, London, 2016)

Rider, S., *These Are the Days of our Lives* (Castle Communications, Chessington, 1993)

St. Michael, M., *Queen in Their Own Words* (Omnibus Press, London, 1992)

West, M., *Queen – The First Ten Years* (Babylon Books, London, 1981)

Recommended websites:
www.brianmay.com
www.queenarchives.com
www.queenconcerts.com
www.queencuttings.com
www.queenmusichall.cz
www.queenonline.com
www.queenpedia.com
www.queenrecordings.com
www.queensongs.info
www.queenvault.com
www.queenzone.com
www.setlist.fm
www.ultimatequeen.co.uk

The Perfect Queen Playlist
'Great King Rat' (1973)
'The March of the Black Queen [Deep Cuts version]' (recorded 1974)
'Nevermore' (1974)
'Tenement Funster' - 'Flick of the Wrist' - 'Lily of the Valley' (1974)
'You're My Best Friend' (1975)
'Bohemian Rhapsody' (1975)
'The Prophet's Song' (1975)
'White Queen (As It Began) [Live at Hammersmith Odeon, London]' (recorded 1975)
'Somebody to Love' (1976)
'You Take My Breath Away' (1976)
'It's Late' (1977)
'Bicycle Race' (1977)
'Don't Stop Me Now' (1978)
'Love of My Life [Live at Festhalle, Frankfurt]' (recorded 1979)
'Under Pressure' (1980)
'Was It All Worth It?' (1989)
'Innuendo' (1991)
'Don't Try So Hard' (1991)
'The Show Must Go On' (1991)
'It's a Beautiful Day [Ross Robertson / DJ Koma remix]' (2005)

Also from Sonicbond Publishing

On Track series
Emerson Lake and Palmer
Mike Goode ISBN: 978-1-78952-000-2

Deep Purple and Rainbow 1968-79
Steve Pilkington ISBN: 978-1-78952-002-6

Yes
Stephen LambeISBN: 978-1-78952-001-9

Blue Oyster Cult
Jacob Holm Lupo ISBN: 978-1-78952-007-1

The Beatles
Andrew Wild ISBN: 978-1-78952-009-5

Roy Wood and the Move
James R Turner ISBN: 978-1-78952-008-8

Genesis
Stuart MacFarlane ISBN: 978-1-78952-005-7

Jethro Tull
Jordan Blum ISBN: 978-1-78952-016-3

The Rolling Stones 1963-80
Steve Pilkington ISBN: 978-1-78952-017-0

On Screen series
Carry On...
Stephen Lambe ISBN: 978-1-78952-004-0

Seinfeld
Stephen Lambe ISBN: 978-1-78952-012-5

Audrey Hepburn
Ellen Cheshire ISBN: 978-1-78952-011-8

Powell and Pressburger
Sam Proctor ISBN: 978-1-78952-013-2

Dad's Army
Huw Lloyd- Jones ISBN: 978-1-78952-015-6

and many more to come!